DEBATING THE CIVIL RIGHTS MOVEMENT, 1945–1968

Debating Twentieth-Century America
Series Editor: James T. Patterson, Brown University

DEBATING THE CIVIL RIGHTS MOVEMENT, 1945–1968

Second Edition

STEVEN F. LAWSON
and
CHARLES PAYNE

Introduction by James T. Patterson

ROWMAN & LITTLEFIELD PUBLISHERS, INC.
Lanham • Boulder • New York • Toronto • Oxford

For Joseph A. Borome and Henry Hampton
—*SFL*
For C. L. R. James and Ella Baker
—*CP*

Permission to reprint the material in the <u>Documents</u> sections is gratefully acknowledged.

ROWMAN & LITTLEFIELD PUBLISHERS, INC.

Published in the United States of America
by Rowman & Littlefield Publishers, Inc.
A wholly owned subsidary of
The Rowman & Littlefield Publishing Group, Inc.
4501 Forbes Boulevard, Suite 200, Lanham, Maryland 20706
www.rowmanlittlefield.com

PO Box 317
Oxford
OX2 9RU, UK

Copyright © 2006 by Rowman & Littlefield Publishers, Inc.

British Library Cataloguing in Publication Information Available

Library of Congress Cataloging-in-Publication Data
Lawson, Steven F., 1945–
    Debating the civil rights movement, 1945–1968 / Steven F. Lawson and Charles Payne.— 2nd ed.
        p.   cm.— (Debating twentieth-century America)
    Includes bibliographical references and index.
    ISBN-13: 978-0-7425-5109-1 (pbk. : alk. paper)
    ISBN-10: 0-7425-5109-1 (pbk. : alk. paper)
1. African Americans—Civil rights—History—20th century—
Sources.   2. African Americans—Civil rights—Historiography.
3. Civil rights movements—United States—History—20th century—
Sources.   4. Civil rights movements—United States—Historiography.
5. United States—Race relations—Sources.   6. United States—Race
relations—Historiography.   I. Payne, Charles M.   II. Title.   III. Series.
    E185.61.L377   2006
    323.1′196073—dc22   2006002135

Printed in the United States of America

♾ ™ The paper used in this publication meets the minimum requirements of American National Standard for Information Sciences—Permanence of Paper for Printed Library Materials, ANSI Z39.48–1992.

CONTENTS

Debating the Civil Rights Movement: The View from the Trenches

Charles Payne

Documents

FOREWORD

Debating Twentieth-Century America is a series of books aimed at helping readers appreciate an important aspect of the writing of history: there is no simple, wholly agreed-on "truth" that captures what has happened in the past. Our understanding of the events of history depends considerably on the way that individual historians interpret them.

With this in mind, each book in the series features two essays, written from varying perspectives, about an important issue, event, or trend in twentieth-century American history. The essayists, who are well-known writers and teachers in their fields, bring to this task considerable expertise. They have delved into the primary and secondary sources and have arrived at personal interpretations of their subjects. Their conclusions, however, reflect different approaches or conclusions. Placed side by side, as in this book, the essays frequently engage in "debate" over the past.

The sources for the essays in this book are far too numerous and varied to reprint in full here. Still, the writers of the essays in *Debating Twentieth-Century America* wish to give readers a sense of the evidence for their generalizations. They therefore include a small number of documents that have influenced their thinking. Readers may find it challenging to evaluate the relevance and importance of these documents.

We hope that the essays and documents will help readers understand the complexity of the past, as well as the subjective process of writing history that carries the past to the present.

James T. Patterson

INTRODUCTION

James T. Patterson

F ew developments of twentieth-century United States history are as controversial—or as important—as the quest for racial justice, or the civil rights movement, as we often call it, that gathered strength in midcentury and peaked in the 1960s. The struggle against white supremacy, as Charles Payne labels racial segregation, featured a host of angry activists, well-meaning white liberals, and determined defenders of the old ways. It produced soaring rhetoric, acts of astonishing personal courage, and a fair amount of violence and bloodshed. All Americans today live in a society that is much affected by these exciting, polarizing events.

Both Payne and Steven F. Lawson are leading historians of race relations and the civil rights movement. In their lively, well-argued essays, they introduce and evaluate many key figures: African-American activists such as Martin Luther King, Jr., A. Philip Randolph, Ella Baker, Septima Clark, and Malcolm X; presidents Harry Truman, Dwight Eisenhower, John Kennedy, and Lyndon Johnson; and defenders of racial discrimination such as Eugene "Bull" Connor of Birmingham, Governor George Wallace of Alabama, and Jim Clark of Selma. Payne and Lawson also weave many exciting events into their narratives—the Montgomery Movement of 1955–1956, the struggle for desegregation of schools in Little Rock, the extraordinary spread of sit-ins, the bloody freedom rides, passage of the historic civil rights acts of 1964 and 1965, the urban riots of the 1960s, and the rise of "Black power."

Readers will discover that Payne and Lawson, who are sophisticated and careful scholars, agree on some aspects of the fight for change in

1

race relations in the 1940s, 1950s, and 1960s. But they look at many of the same events from different perspectives. And they lock horns here and there on a question that has engaged many writers in this thriving field of historical scholarship: how much importance should we attach to "top-down" actors—presidents, the Supreme Court justices, leaders such as King—as contrasted to the doings of unsung activists, including women, sharecroppers, blue-collar workers, and young people at the grass roots? An obviously related set of questions concerns the emphasis we should place on white people's role in the movement. Were they "indispensable" to change, as one of our essayists contends, or for the most part carried along by the dynamic of a movement led by Black people?

The authors also offer shrewd evaluations of the effect of the civil rights movement. Here, too, their perspectives differ in emphasis. Looking back on the dramatic activities of the 1960s, can we conclude that much was accomplished for and by African Americans? Or should we emphasize the long distance that remains to be traveled before the United States makes good on its promises of liberty and justice for all? The arguments of Lawson and Payne, and the documents that they attach to bolster their interpretations, can help us appreciate the controversial nature of events that greatly affect us still.

DEBATING THE CIVIL RIGHTS MOVEMENT: THE VIEW FROM THE NATION

Steven F. Lawson

The federal government played an indispensable role in shaping the fortunes of the civil rights revolution. It is impossible to understand how Blacks achieved first-class citizenship rights in the South without concentrating on what national leaders in Washington, D.C., did to influence the course of events leading to the extension of racial equality. Powerful presidents, congressional lawmakers, and members of the Supreme Court provided the legal instruments to challenge racial segregation and disfranchisement. Without their crucial support, the struggle against white supremacy in the South still would have taken place but would have lacked the power and authority to defeat state governments intent on keeping Blacks in subservient positions.

Along with national officials, the fate of the civil rights movement depended on the presence of national organizations. Groups such as the National Association for the Advancement of Colored People (NAACP), founded in 1909, drew on financial resources and legal talent from all over the country to press the case for equal rights in Congress and the courts. In similar fashion, Dr. Martin Luther King, Jr., and the Southern Christian Leadership Conference (SCLC), established in the mid-1950s, focused their attention on spotlighting white southern racism before a national audience to mobilize support for their side. Even if white Americans outside the South had wanted to ignore the plight of southern Blacks, NAACP lawyers and lobbyists, SCLC protesters, and

3

their like-minded allies made that choice impossible. They could do what Black residents of local communities could not do alone: turn the civil rights struggle into a national cause for concern and prod the federal government into throwing its considerable power to overturn the entrenched system of white domination that had prevailed for centuries in the South.

Historical accounts that center on the national state in Washington and the operations of national organizations take on a particular narrative. The story begins with World War II, which stimulated Black protests against racism, and winds its way through the presidencies of Franklin D. Roosevelt, Harry S. Truman, Dwight D. Eisenhower, John F. Kennedy, and Lyndon B. Johnson. This period witnessed significant presidential executive orders promulgating desegregation in the military and in housing, five pieces of pioneering civil rights legislation, and landmark Supreme Court rulings toppling segregationist practices and extending the right to vote. The familiar geographical signposts of civil rights demonstrations—Montgomery, Birmingham, Selma, Albany, Little Rock—derive their greatest importance as places that molded the critical national debate on ending racial discrimination.

Overall, a nuanced account of the Black freedom struggle requires an interconnected approach. A balanced portrayal acknowledges that Black activists had important internal resources at their disposal, derived from religious, economic, educational, and civic institutions, with which to make their demands. But it does not belittle African-American creativity and determination to conclude that given existing power relationships heavily favoring whites, southern Blacks could not possibly eliminate racial inequality without outside federal assistance. Furthermore, Washington officials had to protect African Americans from intimidation and violence to allow them to carry out their challenges to discrimination. Without this room for maneuvering, civil rights advocates would encounter insurmountable hurdles in confronting white power.

At the same time, the federal government could shape the direction of the struggle by choosing whether and when to respond to Black protest and by deciding on whom to bestow its support within Black communities. Although united around the struggle against white supremacy, African Americans were not monolithic in their outlook and held various shades of opinion on how best to combat racial bias. By allocating precious resources and conferring recognition on particular elements within local Black communities, national leaders could accelerate or slow down the pace of racial change.

PRESIDENT FRANKLIN D. ROOSEVELT AND WORLD WAR II

It is impossible to put a specific date on the opening of the civil rights movement, but World War II contributed greatly to its birth. The war made it difficult for President Franklin D. Roosevelt to ignore Black demands for equal treatment. Fighting a war against Nazism, Hitler's German brand of racism, the United States could not easily defend discrimination within its own borders. Even before the United States officially entered the war in December 1941, African Americans pressured the president to live up to his democratic pronouncements of preserving freedom. The Black labor leader, A. Philip Randolph, head of the Brotherhood of Sleeping Car Porters, threatened to mobilize an all-Black, mass march on Washington scheduled for June to protest racial segregation in the armed forces and discrimination by businesses that received government contracts. Seeking to avoid the political embarrassment of a hostile demonstration at a time when he was preparing the nation to join the Allied side in the war overseas, the president deflected the march by striking a compromise with Randolph. He issued an executive order creating the Fair Employment Practice Committee (FEPC) to investigate job discrimination in federal employment and in industries performing government work. This agency had no enforcement power to follow up its investigations, but by publicizing instances of racial bias, it encouraged a slight increase of employment opportunities for Blacks.

Randolph did not get all he wanted, as the president refused to take action to desegregate the military. Even so, he had created an important model for further civil rights protests. Large-scale demonstrations would be deployed to confront racial discrimination head-on. At this early stage, Randolph realized that African Americans would have to pressure federal officials from the president on down if their efforts to achieve civil rights were to succeed. Despite its limited response, the federal government did use its authority to create an agency to monitor racial bias directly, setting the pattern for future action. The chief executive also set the precedent that most of his successors would follow: he acted mainly to avoid a specific crisis and sought to keep change to a minimum.

The war brought other aid from the federal government, the most significant of which came from the Supreme Court. In 1941, less than 5 percent of adult Blacks in the South had managed to register to vote. In addition to literacy tests and poll taxes, white primaries blocked the overwhelming majority of Blacks from casting ballots. As a legacy of the Civil War, the Republican Party, the party of Abraham Lincoln and emancipation, had relatively little strength in the South and regularly lost at the polls. Whoever triumphed in the Democratic primaries usually won office, and by barring Blacks from participation in these crucial party contests, Democrats excluded them from the only meaningful election taking place. Spearheaded by the NAACP, Texas Blacks organized to support litigation, charging that the state's lily-white Democratic primary violated the Fifteenth Amendment's provision against depriving citizens of the right to vote based on race. In the 1944 ruling of *Smith v. Allwright*, the Supreme Court agreed with the Texas plaintiffs and ordered the Democrats to open their primaries to African Americans.

This landmark opinion helped stimulate a rise in Black voter registration. Three years after the verdict, 12 percent of eligible Blacks in the South had placed their names on the voter rolls, and by 1952, the figure had jumped to 20 percent. The judicial branch of the federal government had knocked out one of the cornerstones of southern disfranchisement. By interpreting the law to the advantage of African Americans, the high tribunal provided the legal support necessary for Black communities to mount successful voter registration drives. Led by NAACP branches, civic associations, labor union affiliates, and churches, Black southerners made the first great strides toward regaining an effective voice in electoral politics.

Despite their successes, they would have accomplished more had it not been for the continued application of suffrage requirements, such as literacy tests, by local white registrars intent on keeping Blacks from voting. The white primary decision as well as the creation of the FEPC showed how critical federal involvement was to the civil rights cause, but they also demonstrated that Washington preferred to act in piecemeal fashion rather than in a comprehensive manner to eliminate the broad array of Jim Crow practices. To this end, Black litigants, lobbyists, community organizers, and protesters would have to continue to prod the national government into action.

THE POSTWAR SOUTH AND PRESIDENT HARRY S. TRUMAN

Conditions in the postwar South underscored the need for federal action. Many Black soldiers returned home determined to pursue their civil rights after having fought for freedom abroad. They joined groups such as the NAACP and organized voter registration drives to take advantage of the Supreme Court's decision in the white primary case. Meeting with some victories as the suffrage rolls began to grow, they nevertheless encountered opposition from southern politicians, reinforced by a murderous reign of terror from white supremacists. As a result, Black leaders looked to the federal government for assistance.

In President Harry S. Truman, Roosevelt's successor from Missouri, they found someone ready to move forward, albeit cautiously, on civil rights. When a delegation of Black leaders and their white allies urged President Truman to investigate the violence spreading throughout the South in 1946, he seemed appalled by the problem and inclined to do something. At the same time, casting an eye toward his presidential campaign in 1948, Truman sought to shore up support among African-American voters, an electorate that was rapidly expanding in the northern states with large numbers of presidential electoral votes. Thus, a combination of moral repugnance against anti-Black violence and political realism prompted the chief executive to create the President's Committee on Civil Rights.

In 1947, the committee issued a far-reaching report. *To Secure These Rights* contained bold proposals that would give the federal government increased power to combat racial inequality. It called for desegregation of the armed forces, interstate transportation, and government employment; recommended the cessation of federal aid to segregated institutions; proposed measures to challenge lynching and voting discrimination; called for legislation to resurrect the FEPC, which southern congressmen had succeeded in killing; suggested the creation of a Civil Rights Division in the Justice Department to prosecute violations of civil rights offenses more vigorously; and advocated to establish a Civil Rights

Commission to investigate ongoing problems. Taken together, these proposals sketched out the liberal agenda on civil rights for the next twenty years. Black and white reformers assumed that racism troubled the American conscience because it conflicted with basic democratic principles of equal treatment under law.

Liberals, however, overestimated the willingness of southern whites to see their way of life as immoral or hypocritical and accept corrective measures along the lines of the committee's report. In fact, in 1948, when Truman sent Congress specific civil rights legislation to follow up on his agency's recommendations, southern Democrats raised a barrage of criticism that stunned the president. Fearful that the angry South would defect from his upcoming campaign for the presidency, he quickly backtracked and refrained from pushing the measures he had only so recently endorsed.

Try as he might, this presidential Aladdin could not push the civil rights genie back in the bottle. The racially progressive forces that had been gathering strength since World War II refused to retreat. From within the Democratic Party, white liberals led by Hubert H. Humphrey insisted that Truman embrace once again the program he had proposed and then abandoned in face of southern opposition. These dissidents succeeded in writing the main elements of *To Secure These Rights* into the Democratic presidential platform of 1948 and convinced Truman to run on them. By this time, the shrewd incumbent had adopted the campaign strategy of reaching out to northern Black voters who could wield the balance of power in securing his election. For example, Truman issued an executive order that paved the way toward ending racial segregation in the armed forces, a demand originally raised by A. Philip Randolph seven years earlier. Though white southerners grumbled and some even backed the independent party candidate from their region, South Carolina's Strom Thurmond, Truman counted on most of them holding to tradition and supporting the Democratic Party. Indeed, these calculations proved accurate, and Harry Truman won election to another term.

Having thrown federal support behind civil rights, President Truman also showed the limitations of the nation's commitment to combating racism. As he had done the previous year, in 1949 Truman introduced his civil rights program into Congress only to suffer the same fate. With southern Democrats occupying key positions in the legislature, the administration's civil rights proposals did not get very far. The prospect of a filibuster in the Senate—unlimited debate that could only be terminated by a two-thirds majority—deterred civil rights proponents from vigorously waging a fight. Furthermore, the president hesitated to make a greater effort to break the legislative stalemate for fear of antagonizing southern Democrats whose votes he needed for funding his increasingly expensive Cold War measures to contain communist expansion.

THE IMPACT OF THE COLD WAR

The Cold War had a much higher priority on the president's agenda than did civil rights. Once the country became involved in the Korean War in 1950, the chief executive focused his attention mainly on that conflict for the rest of his term, thereby sacrificing the possibility of passing civil rights legislation. Nevertheless, African Americans tried to exploit Cold War rhetoric for any ideological advantage they might gain in their struggle for freedom. As long as the United States sanctioned racial discrimination, it remained vulnerable to charges from the Soviet Union that while preaching freedom and democracy in foreign affairs, it did not practice either at home. In their struggle for world power with the United States, the Soviets exploited racial incidents in the South to win over allies, especially among emerging nonwhite nations in Asia and Africa. As a matter of fact, the President's Committee on Civil Rights, which shaped so much of Truman's proposals, had acknowledged this problem in its landmark report: "An American diplomat cannot argue for free elections in foreign lands without meeting the challenge that in sections of America qualified voters do not have access to the polls."

Despite the nation's lofty, democratic pronouncements, the Cold War worked against civil rights advancement. Truman's policy of containing the Soviet Union overseas fueled attempts to check communism at home. "Red Scare" hysteria blurred the line between government attempts to defend the nation against espionage and attacks on Americans whose views were deemed too radical. Spies were fair game, but in the South, civil rights activists who challenged segregation and disfranchisement were also denounced as subversives.

In this way, important alternatives for pursuing the Black freedom struggle were shut off. Labor unions would have provided a vehicle for change. In the South the Congress of Industrial Organizations (CIO) tried to organize Black and white workers after World War II. An affiliate in Winston-Salem succeeded in establishing an interracial union of tobacco workers until the R. J. Reynolds Company fought back by using charges of communism as a weapon to discredit and destroy the CIO affiliate. Had the union triumphed, it would have opened the way for providing Blacks with crucial economic leverage to fight against racism and for placing economic equality on a par with civil and political rights on the freedom agenda. With this option closed, traditional civil rights groups such as the NAACP continued to shape the struggle more as a means of achieving constitutional rights than attacking economic inequalities based on class as well as racial exploitation. Ironically, the NAACP, which expelled Communists from its organization, nevertheless found itself the target of "Red-baiting" by southern white conservatives, who considered it no less subversive of the established racial and social order than labor unions.

THE SUPREME COURT AND SCHOOL DESEGREGATION

Although the national government's Cold War policies helped limit choices for the civil rights movement, the Truman administration and its liberal allies managed to advance the cause. With Congress deadlocked, the president and the NAACP shifted the battle to the courts. Led by attorneys for the NAACP, Black plaintiffs attacked racially restrictive covenants—deeds limiting sales to Caucasians only—that frustrated housing desegregation and won their case before the Supreme Court in *Shelley v. Kraemer* in 1948. In pleading this and subsequent cases, the NAACP had the assistance of Truman's Justice Department, which filed *amicus curiae* (friend of the court) briefs.

Two years later, the National Association struck at Jim Crow in higher education. Its chief counsel, Thurgood Marshall, argued that by setting up dual law schools at the University of Texas and segregated graduate facilities at the University of Oklahoma, these state institutions, like those elsewhere in the South, had created separate but not equal opportunities for African Americans. In *Sweatt v. Painter* and *McLaurin v. Board of Regents*, the high tribunal agreed and suggested that increased financial resources to upgrade Black schools could not produce genuine equality, that Black students would have to receive the chance to learn in an environment that did not treat them as inferior. These decisions did not overturn segregation squarely, but they did set the stage for the NAACP to challenge the doctrine of separate but equal head-on in the field of public school education, which would affect white and Black southerners more profoundly than any other challenge thus far.

The assault on public school segregation highlights the crucial role played by the federal government in pushing forward the struggle for civil rights. Initiated by the NAACP and supported by its local branches, the litigation to desegregate the schools culminated in *Brown v. Board of Education*, a series of five cases from (Topeka) Kansas, South Carolina, Virginia, Delaware, and Washington, D.C. In 1954, the Supreme Court put to rest the legal fiction that under a system of enforced racial separation Black students could receive an equal education. Speaking for the high tribunal, Chief Justice Earl Warren did not attack white supremacy directly or castigate southerners for historically oppressing African Americans. Rather, he argued that it was impossible for Blacks to obtain the full benefits of an education under the system of segregation. "We conclude," he asserted, "that in the field of public education the doctrine of 'separate but equal' has no place. Separate educational facilities are inherently unequal."

Although this case pertained solely to public schools, the unanimous Supreme Court justices infused the overall fight for civil rights with constitutional legitimacy. They raised doubts about the validity of segregation as a means of preserving white supremacy. Jim Crow did not automatically crumble, and many obstacles remained; however, the highest federal court in the land had raised a powerful voice on behalf of racial equality and given Blacks hope that the national government was on their side. At the same time, the court demonstrated that it had the power to influence the timing of desegregation. In a follow-up decision in 1955, the justices ruled that the states did not have to rush to integrate their schools; rather, they could do so "with all deliberate speed." This imprecise phrase reflected the judges' desire to avoid inflaming racial tensions that might result from forcing the states to abandon immediately a system that had existed for nearly a century. Moreover, they left it up to federal district courts, those most closely situated in the states involved, to approve the timetable for desegregation. Under these circumstances, a bold judicial opinion had turned excessively cautious. As one commentator sarcastically remarked, the ruling permitted the southern states "to make haste slowly," thereby keeping school desegregation to a minimum. It would take another fourteen years for the judiciary to find that the pace of school desegregation was moving too slowly and order a swift end to further attempts at delay.

MASSIVE RESISTANCE

Given this breathing space, southern whites embarked on a campaign of massive resistance to *Brown*. In doing so, the states in Dixie recognized how high the Court had raised Black expectations for freedom. Consequently, they sought to contain the efforts of their Black residents to secure the judiciary's promise of equality. The efforts of obstructionist whites received aid and comfort from the South's congressional representatives in Washington, who, in 1956, issued a manifesto pledging to overturn the court's landmark ruling. Calling the *Brown* opinion "a clear abuse of judicial power," the 101 signers of the pronouncement vowed "to use all lawful means to bring about a reversal of this decision."

However, some southern extremists went beyond legal methods to preserve Jim Crow. The year after *Brown* witnessed several highly publicized murders of Blacks, perhaps the most repulsive of which occurred in Mississippi with the brutal murder of Emmett Till. A fourteen-year-old from Chicago visiting relatives in the Magnolia State in the summer of 1955, he allegedly made offensive remarks to a white woman store clerk. Her husband and brother-in-law retaliated by killing Till and dropping his body into the Tallahatchie River. The crime was prosecuted, but an all-white jury quickly acquitted the defendants, who after the trial brazenly admitted their guilt to a journalist in return for a cash fee.

PRESIDENT DWIGHT D. EISENHOWER

By this time Dwight D. Eisenhower occupied the White House. Taking office in 1953, the president sent mixed signals to southern authorities that encouraged their resistance. Had President Eisenhower, a former

Army general and beloved hero of World War II, chosen to speak out forcefully on behalf of racial equality, he would likely have served as a moderating influence and undercut the strength of massive resistance. However, by temperament and belief, he chose not to.

Eisenhower considered gradualism as the best method for lessening racial bias. He expressed doubts about using the stick of legislation to force the South into submission, questioning whether "cold lawmaking" would have a lasting effect. Rather, the chief executive preferred to dangle the carrots of education, mutual respect, and prayer to address the problem of racial bias. Given these sentiments, it is not surprising that Eisenhower refused to speak out strongly in support of the *Brown* decision. He endorsed the ruling as the law of the land, but he would not take a moral stand in defense of the Court's opinion. By shirking his responsibility to back desegregation fully and firmly, the president tacitly encouraged the southern states to evade compliance with *Brown*.

However, Eisenhower's sympathy for the South did not keep him from recognizing authority in the federal government to remedy racial injustice. He spoke out for removing discriminatory barriers to Black suffrage. Unlike southern school desegregation, the president considered protection from discrimination in exercising the ballot as constitutionally guaranteed and central to the system of representative government upon which the nation was founded. Eisenhower further reasoned that once southern Blacks recovered the vote, they could peacefully and deliberately use it to relieve other racial ills. Eventually, this would remove the burden from the federal government for having to intervene in disputes between white and Black southerners. This outlook also reflected Eisenhower's gradualist philosophy; changes through use of the ballot would come slowly, thereby allowing the South time to accept alterations in long-standing racial practices.

THE MONTGOMERY BUS BOYCOTT

Black southerners refused to abide by Eisenhower's gradualist timetable. In Montgomery, Alabama, the "Cradle of the Confederacy," a number of Black groups were promoting voter registration and planning challenges to discriminatory service on city buses. On December 1, 1955, Rosa Parks, a middle-aged Black seamstress, refused to vacate her seat for a white passenger who boarded the bus on which she was riding home after a long day's work. The arrest of this mild-mannered woman sparked a one-year boycott of the buses. A network of local organizations made this protest possible. Parks was an official of the Montgomery chapter of the NAACP, and the president of her branch, E. D. Nixon, arranged for her release from jail and called for a demonstration. The Women's Political Council, led by Jo Ann Gibson Robinson, a college professor, then plotted strategy for a one-day boycott and distributed thousands of flyers to alert people to the plan. They recruited clergy to lend their churches for mass meetings and encourage their congregants to withhold patronage from the buses. They also tapped a relatively new minister in town, the twenty-six-year-old Reverend Martin Luther King, Jr., to head the Montgomery Improvement Association, the coalition established to coordinate the protest.

The year-long campaign showed the growing power of a grassroots movement, but it also proved that the struggle for civil rights desperately needed the federal government to crack determined white southern opposition. By mid-1956, the city still refused to capitulate to Black demands despite the severe economic losses inflicted by the boycott and defections by some white women who drove their maids to work. Coinciding with the boycott, the NAACP had initiated a lawsuit challenging the validity of government-sanctioned bus segregation. In June, the federal district court ruled for the Black plaintiffs; in November, the Supreme Court affirmed the decision. Only after the high tribunal spoke did Montgomery finally abandon segregation on its bus lines. The boycott played a necessary part in pointing the way toward freedom, but without the legal backing of the federal government, it proved an insufficient means of ending Jim Crow.

THE CIVIL RIGHTS ACT OF 1957

The same situation applied to expanding the right to vote. Washington responded when Black needs fit into the calculations of white politicians. Eisenhower saw suffrage as the most important and least objectionable goal of civil rights advocates. Shortly before the presidential election of 1956, Attorney General Herbert Brownell crafted a comprehensive civil rights proposal aimed at encouraging school desegregation and challenging suffrage violations in the courts. Eisenhower's victory strengthened his desire to introduce the measure into Congress, for the president had won increased electoral support from African Americans. Though the majority of Black voters backed Adlai Stevenson, the Democratic nominee, the popular Eisenhower made significant Republican inroads among African Americans.

The Civil Rights Act of 1957 was transformed mainly into a piece of suffrage legislation owing to the efforts of the president and Democratic leaders in Congress. Eisenhower backed away from supporting the section of his administration's bill that authorized the Justice Department to file school desegregation cases. In accordance with his own personal and political beliefs, the chief executive did not want to get involved in educational issues and chose instead to concentrate on giving the attorney general power to bring cases in federal court to stop voter registrars from discriminating against qualified Black voters. He also endorsed provisions creating a Civil Rights Division in the Justice Department to strengthen its enforcement powers and an independent Civil Rights Commission to investigate racial problems and recommend solutions. These proposals had first been sketched out by Truman's Committee on Civil Rights, and Eisenhower signed them into law.

At the same time, Senate Democratic majority leader Lyndon B. Johnson of Texas threw his party's support behind the legislation. The lawmaker from Texas had his own presidential ambitions, but the fact that as a southerner he had opposed civil rights legislation in the past hurt his chances for nomination with northern white liberals and Black Democrats. He also recognized the recent gains Eisenhower had made among the Black electorate and sought to lessen their impact by avoiding a tough battle over the administration's civil rights proposal that would split the northern and southern wings of his party. Consequently, the Texas senator helped broker an agreement that kept his southern colleagues from waging a long and bitter filibuster that would have hurt the party's and the majority leader's standing among African Americans. This agreement guaranteed passage of the modified civil rights bill Eisenhower had come to support, which eliminated references to the more controversial issue of school integration.

The first national law on civil rights enacted since Reconstruction had only a modest effect on enfranchising southern Blacks. The reliance on litigation by lawyers in the Civil Rights Division as provided in the statute proved time-consuming and cumbersome. Bringing suits against registrars on a county-by-county basis created broad room for evasion through appeals and delays. In addition, because the cases were heard before federal judges in the South, Black interests as represented by the Justice Department did not always get a sympathetic hearing.

The other agency created by the 1957 Act, the Civil Rights Commission, underscored the need to revise the federal government's strategy. In 1958, the commission held hearings in Montgomery, Alabama. Black citizens described how white registrars denied their applications no matter how qualified they were to vote. As a result, the next year the commission issued a far-reaching report that urged the president and Congress to scuttle reliance on the judiciary and approve a plan to send federal registrars into those recalcitrant southern communities that discriminated against potential Black voters. Like the Truman Committee's *To Secure These Rights,* the Civil Rights Commission's report suggested the path the government would eventually follow. However, in the short run, lawmakers proved unwilling to shift direction, though in 1960 they passed another civil rights act that corrected some of the technical defects in the earlier legislation. Washington had shown a capacity to act under the right political circumstances, but its efforts still left 70 percent of Black southerners unable to exercise the franchise in 1960.

LITTLE ROCK

Nor had the federal government accomplished much in aid of school desegregation. Refusing to use the White House as a moral pulpit to preach compliance with *Brown,* Eisenhower stood by as southern officials thwarted the decision—that is, until Little Rock. In 1957, the NAACP had won a federal court decree to desegregate Central High School in the Arkansas capital. Led by Daisy Bates, the association's local president, nine Black youths set out in September to attend school with whites for the first time in their lives. They found their way blocked by Governor Orval Faubus, who posted the national guard around campus to keep the Black students from entering the school. When Eisenhower met with the governor and warned him not to defy the federal court order, Faubus pulled the troops. By this time, however, the governor had inflamed racial passions beyond the boiling point; and when the

Little Rock Nine attempted to enter the high school, they were turned back by raging mobs.

Faced with this obvious challenge to the federal government, Eisenhower had little choice but to respond with force. The former five-star general dispatched the 101st Airborne Division to Little Rock to preserve the peace and assure the safety of Black students seeking to enter Central. In this episode Eisenhower revealed the enormous might of the federal government while also exposing the reluctance of presidents to deploy it. Concerned about overstepping the boundaries imposed by the Constitution's division of powers between national and state governments, the chief executive had allowed Arkansas as much leeway as possible and intervened only when Washington's authority came under direct attack. Whatever reluctance to use force Eisenhower had shown, his resolution of the crisis had inspired optimism among African Americans. Roger Wilkins, a civil rights activist and scholar who was twenty-five years old at the time, recalled, "Little Rock was a major milestone. We felt the country was becoming more just and the federal government was on our side."

Nevertheless, this incident showed that the national government remained a tentative ally for African Americans. Whatever rights the Constitution guaranteed and the courts affirmed, the federal government was likely to act only if pressured to do so. Events such as Little Rock thus shaped an understandable crisis mentality among civil rights proponents. Appeals to moral conscience went only so far in persuading white officials to combat Jim Crow. Presidents and members of Congress responded to grievances more effectively when Blacks and their white allies exerted substantial political pressure or when their attempts to obtain equality provoked violence from white resisters. In other words, national lawmakers were more likely to respond to the threat of possible racial firestorms than to abstract appeals to justice. In this way, the government helped shape the logic for protest by signaling to Blacks the need to confront racism head-on before Washington would choose to intervene.

MARTIN LUTHER KING, JR.

Martin Luther King, Jr., was slowly making his way to this conclusion during the 1950s. Following the Montgomery bus boycott, King had created the Southern Christian Leadership Conference in 1957. Consisting mainly of Black ministers, the organization operated as "the political arm of the Black church" and reflected King's commitment to nonviolent direct action as a technique to battle all forms of racism. Not only did the Reverend King seek to convert the hearts and minds of white racists through appeals to their Christian consciences, but he and his followers recognized the necessity of applying political pressure to change racist behavior and practices. Accordingly, Black communities would have to mount sustained mass demonstrations to confront Jim Crow directly, bring the evil of racism out in the open, and goad reforms from white authorities.

In the years after Montgomery, King's efforts came up short. By 1960, massive resistance in the South had kept Black enfranchisement to a minimum and blocked desegregation of public schools and other facilities almost entirely. The federal government had provided some relief through passage of two civil rights acts, but Washington officials preferred that Black citizens voluntarily work out settlements with southern politicians. In taking this approach, national leaders helped to structure the civil rights struggle by forcing Black southerners to devise creative tactics to confront white supremacy. Deprived of the right to vote, Blacks mobilized the resource most readily available to them—they put their bodies on the line against racism.

STUDENT ACTIVISM

The Little Rock Nine highlighted the important role played by students in challenging segregation, but the wave of sit-ins hurled high school– and college-age youngsters into the vanguard of the movement. Whereas adults had initiated and controlled the legal battles over school desegregation, the younger generation moved to the forefront in confronting Jim Crow directly along a broad front. Sparked by the sit-in protest of four college students to desegregate lunch counters in Greensboro, North Carolina, in February 1960, the movement spread within the year to over two hundred cities and involved thousands of participants. These youthful demonstrators nevertheless had significant adult support. Advisers to NAACP Youth Councils offered valuable assistance as did civil rights veterans such as Ella Baker. Miss Baker, as she was respectfully called, served as an official of SCLC in 1960 and was instrumental in convening a conference of student sit-in activists, which met in Raleigh, North Carolina, in April. Out of this gathering came a new protest organization, the Student Nonviolent Coordinating Committee (SNCC, said "Snick,"), which became one of the most imaginative and militant civil rights groups in the 1960s. SNCC members emerged out of the sit-ins not content just to fight for the opportunity to eat a hamburger at a lunch counter in a white-owned store. Rather, they had their eyes on a larger prize: to liberate African Americans from all forms of racial, political, and economic oppression. Hence, they concentrated on working with local Blacks to organize their own communities for freedom.

Though focusing their efforts at the community level, SNCC realized the need to pressure the federal government for assistance, because most local white leaders did not intend to relinquish power voluntarily. SNCC organizers in Atlanta used the 1960 presidential election to dramatize this point. In late October, they persuaded the Reverend King, who had recently moved to Atlanta from Montgomery, to join a sit-in to integrate a restaurant in a downtown department store. The protesters hoped that Dr. King's arrest would create a "national uproar" and force the presidential candidates, Democrat John F. Kennedy and Republican Richard M. Nixon, to take a committed stand that went beyond platitudinous campaign promises of equal opportunity. Their strategy worked. Kennedy spoke out in King's behalf and after complicated behind-the-scenes maneuvering helped arrange the civil rights leader's release from jail. Nixon chose to remain silent on the issue, seeking instead to snare some of the traditionally Democratic southern white votes to the GOP. On election day, most of the Black voters who had defected to Eisenhower in 1956 returned to the Democratic fold and tipped the margin of victory in Kennedy's favor. The new president won by less than 1 percent of the popular vote and with few electoral votes (eighty-four) to spare, underscoring the importance of African-American ballots.

THE KENNEDY ADMINISTRATION

In spite of Kennedy's political debt to Black voters, he started out as a cautious proponent of civil rights. During the campaign he had pledged to wipe out discrimination in federally funded housing as easily as with the stroke of a pen; however, it took him two years to put pen to paper and issue an executive order, which even then was inadequate. The president had also said he would send a comprehensive civil rights program to Congress, but he quickly backed off. As a matter of fact, he shied away from his campaign promises for fear of antagonizing powerful white southern politicans from his own party who exerted influence in the legislature far greater than their numbers. Though a minority, these lawmakers chaired important committees that could bottle up legislation; and in the Senate they wielded the filibuster, or merely threatened its use, to prevent a majority from approving civil rights bills. The chief executive's unwillingness to mount a legislative assault caused King and his allies to reflect that the first two years of the Kennedy administration seemed very much like an extension of Eisenhower's regime.

Indeed, in one important respect it was. The president continued his predecessor's policy of using the Justice Department to file suits under the 1957 Civil Rights Act to challenge discrimination in voter registration procedures. However, Kennedy's civil rights attorneys stepped up their activities in the courts to a far greater extent than in the previous administration. By going through the judiciary, Kennedy hoped to avoid the kind of bruising battle he would face with southern lawmakers if he had vigorously proposed civil rights legislation. The Justice Department, directed by his brother Robert as attorney general, won an impressive number of victories. However, the department would have been even more successful if the president, to satisfy key southern Democratic senators, had not appointed a number of federal district judges who turned out to rule consistently against extending Black voting rights. One such jurist, William Harold Cox of Mississippi, referred to Blacks in open court as "niggers" who acted "like a bunch of chimpanzees."

FREEDOM RIDES

Frustrated with the Kennedy administration's slow pace, civil rights activists stepped up their efforts to produce the kind of crisis that would force the federal government to back them up. In May 1961, they launched "freedom rides" to desegregate bus stations serving interstate travelers. Six months earlier, the Supreme Court had ruled that these facilities must be open to Black passengers, but in the South little seemed to have changed. The Congress of Racial Equality (CORE) intended to see what the president would do about upholding federal law. An interracial group founded in 1942, CORE had conducted a similar protest in 1947. This time, led by James Farmer, the organization "felt [it] could count on the racists of the South to create a crisis so that the federal government would be compelled to enforce the law." The red flag they waved in front of bullheaded southern officials consisted of thirteen Black and white passengers in two buses taking off from Washington, D.C., and headed for New Orleans.

The freedom riders encountered the anticipated response. They met with sporadic opposition along the route until, on May 14, Mother's Day, white mobs attacked one bus as it stopped in Anniston, Alabama, and the other as it pulled into Birmingham. One of the vehicles was firebombed, and on both buses the passengers were chased off, assaulted, and bloodied. The Kennedy administration fretted that this ugly incident would embarrass the president as he embarked on a Cold War meeting in Vienna with the head of the Soviet Union, Nikita Khrushchev. Hence, it urged a "cooling-off period" to forestall further violence. The bus companies were anxious to comply, but civil rights activists refused to yield. SNCC sent in reinforcements to resume the ride, and faced with this unbending determination, the Justice Department arranged for a Greyhound bus to transport the protesters to Montgomery and obtained an agreement from Governor John Patterson to guarantee their safety. This guarantee proved worthless—Patterson considered the riders rabble-rousers and the federal government to be coddling them needlessly—and the riders were attacked once again as they reached the Alabama capital. This time, in addition to several civil rights activists, a Justice Department representative monitoring the scene was severely beaten.

Up to this point Washington had shown itself willing, if not anxious, to defer to state authorities to uphold the law. With one of its own agents wounded and the prospect for further bloodshed escalating, the Kennedy administration finally dispatched federal marshals to help bring peace to Montgomery. The Reverend King returned to the city of his greatest triumph to lend moral support to the freedom riders. After a menacing white mob surrounded the church in which King was holding a rally, marshals battled rioters until Governor Patterson agreed to send state troops to disperse the crowd, end the crisis, and get both the federal government and civil rights demonstrators out of Alabama. Subsequently, Attorney General Kennedy made a deal with Mississippi officials that arranged for the besieged riders to obtain safe passage to their next stop in Jackson, where local police took over and arrested them though without further brutality.

The freedom rides underscore how the national government influenced the direction of civil rights struggles. Reluctant to use force and overstep federal-state boundary lines, national authorities exposed civil rights demonstrators to serious risks. The president bemoaned the obstructionism of Governor Patterson, but he also became "fed up with the Freedom Riders" for not pulling back after the initial violence in Alabama, when "it didn't do any good to go down there." This brand of thinking assumed an unwarranted moral and legal equivalent between peaceful civil rights demonstrators entitled to their rights and state authorities bent on thwarting them. On this occasion, the Kennedy administration's timidity was even more repugnant because the Supreme Court had guaranteed the right to unfettered interstate travel, which the riders were seeking to exercise. Under the pressure of overt and repeated violence, Attorney General Kennedy finally reversed course. Though belatedly and after serious injuries had occurred, he persuaded the Interstate Commerce Commission (ICC) to issue regulations to enforce the court's decree desegregating bus terminals. Not surprisingly, then, civil rights activists reasonably concluded that by provoking crises they could prod the federal government into coercing the white South to fulfill its constitutional obligations toward African-American citizens.

THE ALBANY, GEORGIA, CAMPAIGN

Albany, Georgia, highlighted this point, though the results proved less satisfactory to the civil rights cause. This town of fifty-six thousand people in southwest Georgia's farming country practiced segregation as rigidly as any place else in the region. Yet it also contained a rich network of Black churches, businesses, an NAACP branch, and the campus of Albany State College. These Black institutions provided a basis for waging the civil rights struggle, though early efforts at protest had not panned out. Spurred by the freedom rides, in mid-1961 SNCC organizers entered the city to challenge segregation. They met with little success and ran into conflicts with local Black organizations, particularly the NAACP, whose approach differed from their own. Fighting Jim Crow was tough enough without internal bickering, so to promote unity the Albany Movement was established. A series of nonviolent demonstrations against job discrimination, police brutality, and segregated public facilities, including bus and train terminals, resulted in the arrest of more than one thousand protesters, which stretched the resources of the umbrella organization. Seeking outside help and publicity, the president of the Albany Movement, William Anderson, requested that Martin Luther King and the SCLC furnish assistance.

King seized the opportunity to participate. His group's campaign had largely stalled after the Montgomery bus boycott and direct action initiatives had passed to SNCC and CORE. From December 1961 through July 1962, King went to jail three times along with thousands of others from the Albany Movement, all to no avail. Though the city clearly violated the ICC's order prohibiting segregated interstate transportation facilities, the federal government refused more than token involvement, preferring instead to get the local parties to negotiate a solution. Washington primarily saw its role as responding to breakdowns in law and order, and as long as Albany's police chief Laurie Pritchett gave the public appearance of arresting Black protesters without excessive force, the Kennedy administration stayed mainly on the sidelines. This did not mean that demonstrators avoided instances of police brutality, only that these encounters occurred sporadically and usually remained outside of coverage by the national news media that had convened in Albany.

In effect, the Kennedy administration had contributed to a civil rights defeat. It is true that the Albany Movement never achieved the solidarity necessary to wage a successful struggle against a crafty and united foe. However, by seeking to maintain a position of neutrality, the Kennedys did little to upset the balance of power that left the insurgents, including King, at a decided disadvantage. Furthermore, one of the staunchly segregationist federal district judges the president had appointed, Robert Elliott, hampered the protesters by issuing restraining orders to stop their rallies, thereby slowing down their momentum at critical moments. The Federal Bureau of Investigation (FBI) had agents on the scene to monitor the action, but they failed to protect Black protesters who were clearly seeking to exercise their rights peacefully. This standoffish behavior particularly irked civil rights activists and remained a serious source of contention throughout the entire freedom struggle. "One of the greatest problems we face with the FBI in the South," King complained publicly, "is that the agents are white southerners who have been influenced by the mores of their community. To maintain their status, they have to be friendly with the local police and people who are promoting segregation." Albany taught King to prepare more carefully to assure clear-cut confrontations between civil rights demonstrators and segregationists that would pressure the federal government into making a strong response.

VOTER REGISTRATION

This was precisely what the Kennedy administration hoped to avoid. Concerned with escalating racial conflicts stemming from direct action campaigns, the president sought to cool passions while still pushing the civil rights agenda ahead. One answer seemed to lie in promoting voter registration. A long-standing goal of the freedom struggle, suffrage expansion, also appealed to the chief executive because it involved much quieter methods than did emotionally charged, confrontational demonstrations against Jim Crow. In addition, citizenship training and canvassing door to door to sign up new voters generally attracted far less publicity than sit-ins, marches, and the like. Another incentive came from the fact that since passage of the 1957 Civil Rights Act, the Justice Department had power to file suits against biased voter registration practices. To steer civil rights activities in a safer direction and encourage Blacks to use the ballot as a more acceptable tool of protest, the Kennedy administration orchestrated the creation of the Voter Education Project (VEP), which operated from 1962 to 1964. Under this arrangement, liberal philanthropic foundations financed and the Atlanta-based Southern Regional Council supervised the program to line up new Black voters. The major civil rights organizations—the NAACP, SCLC, SNCC, and CORE—accepted the government's invitation to join the VEP.

Having encouraged civil rights forces to work for suffrage, the federal government nonetheless provided less than full support, once again shaping the outcome of the movement in crucial ways. In making the initial arrangements for the VEP, Justice Department officials had assured civil rights activists that if they fell subject to danger they could rely on Washington for shelter. Once the project got under way, however, voting rights workers in the field, especially those in the rural, isolated South, found little in the way of direct federal protection. The Justice Department might file a lawsuit to stop voting discrimination, but it declined to deploy the FBI or federal marshals to protect civil rights workers from violence. Morally, having made a commitment in the first place, the government should have offered protection. Legally, it had the authority to shield from harm those who were seeking to exercise their constitutional rights. But politically, neither the president nor the attorney general wanted to lose favor with their southern white Democratic political allies. Thus, the Kennedy administration wrapped political considerations in legalistic terms. Its attorneys argued that the federal system of government meant that the states had the chief responsibility for law enforcement and that the FBI was only an investigative branch, not a national police agency. Under these circumstances, the Kennedy administration left voter registration workers at the mercy of the same local police who refused to protect them and frequently engaged in intimidating them.

This policy of encouraging voter registration on the one hand and failing to protect those who promoted it on the other produced mixed results. Between 1962 and 1964, approximately seven hundred thousand southern Blacks successfully added their names to the voter lists, and the percentage of adult Blacks on the registration rolls climbed from 29 to 43. Only in Florida, Tennessee, and Texas, however, did the majority of eligible Blacks manage to register, while in Alabama, Louisiana, and Mississippi less than one-third had qualified to vote. The new voters generally came from towns and cities where restrictions against African Americans were less rigidly applied. In rural areas where Blacks were more isolated and subject to greater repression, the franchise situation scarcely improved.

In Mississippi conditions remained so bad that the VEP chose to suspend operations. In 1964, only 6.7 percent of Black adults in the state could vote, and the prospects for significant improvement appeared slim as long as civil rights workers were harassed and the federal government provided no protection. Against fierce state resistance that included police violence and arrests, Justice Department lawsuits proved inadequate. In ceasing to fund voter registration drives in Mississippi, the VEP lamented the "failure of the federal government to protect the people who have sought to register and vote or who are working actively in getting others to register."

The federal government refused to flex its considerable muscle on a day-to-day basis in the South, but it did respond to extraordinary circumstances. Eisenhower had shown in Little Rock that the national government would intervene to uphold federal authority when it was directly threatened by state resistance. Kennedy followed suit. He preferred to rely on reasonable dialogue with state officials to persuade them to obey the law, but when such conversations proved futile he had no choice but to act forcefully. Such was the case with the University of Mississippi. The federal courts had ordered the state to admit James Meredith as the first Black student at Ole Miss. Governor Ross Barnett, as had Orval Faubus in Arkansas, strung the president along to delay admission. In October 1962, the governor's stalling tactics heightened white resistance, and when Meredith showed up to attend classes a riot erupted on campus. Only then did the president finally run out of patience and send in federal troops to protect Meredith and quell the disturbance, but not before two people died and 375 were injured. Once again, civil rights proponents learned the hard way that if they wanted federal intervention, they would have to produce a crisis that resulted in the breakdown of public order.

BIRMINGHAM

By the spring of 1963 Martin Luther King, Jr., had fully reached this conclusion. One of his aides explained: "To take a moderate approach hoping to get white help, doesn't help. They nail you to the cross, and it saps the enthusiasm of the followers. You've got to have a crisis." He selected Birmingham, Alabama, to provoke federal intervention. The city had a long history of repression of civil rights activists and labor union organizers, and its police commissioner, Eugene "Bull" Connor, used an iron fist to turn back any signs of insurgency. In addition, the Ku Klux Klan and other terrorists had planted bombs to quiet local civil rights proponents such as the Reverend Fred Shuttlesworth, albeit unsuccessfully. Into this cauldron of racial hostility, King brought his troops to stir up the local Black community in a campaign against Jim Crow. Indeed, under Shuttlesworth's fearless direction Birmingham Blacks had already been carrying on protests against segregation, but they had failed to capture the kind of national attention that would force the federal government to render sufficient support.

The protests King spearheaded in April and May sparked federal interest. Unlike King's previous experience in Albany, television cameras and newspaper photographs produced powerful images of peaceful demonstrators suffering brutality at the hands of Bull Connor's law enforcement agents. Snarling police dogs bit demonstrators, and firefighters unleashed high-power water hoses to disperse protesters. Birmingham's jails filled with Black marchers, among them King. When the number of adults available for protest dwindled, King recruited children, some as young as six years old, whose tender age did not keep them from getting assaulted and arrested. Faced with a racial crisis spiraling out of control, the Kennedy administration stepped up its efforts to restore peace. In early May, Justice Department negotiators helped hammer out a settlement that initiated desegregation of restaurants and increased employment opportunities for Blacks. Unfortunately, this agreement did not stop random acts of violence. A few days after the settlement, a bomb exploded at the hotel at which King was staying. Although nobody was hurt, angry Blacks lost patience and pelted police with rocks and bottles. Even more horrible, several months later in September, a more lethal bomb ripped through the basement of a Birmingham church and killed four young Black girls.

THE 1964 CIVIL RIGHTS ACT

Birmingham and scores of other demonstrations throughout the South finally prompted President Kennedy to take a strong stand against segregation and exert leadership on behalf of the Black freedom movement. In early June 1963, he sent federal marshals to ensure that Black students gain entry to the University of Alabama. In a stage-managed and highly publicized affair, Governor George Wallace appeared on campus, voiced his objections in front of the administration building, and then stepped aside in the face of superior federal might. But Kennedy's greatest performance came in a nationally televised address to the American people. On the evening of June 11, he spoke powerfully about the ethical imperative of providing African Americans with first-class citizenship. Civil rights was "a moral issue," he proclaimed, "as old as the Scriptures and . . . as clear as the Constitution." Deeply concerned that the "fires of frustration and discord are burning in every city," the president warned that burgeoning racial crises "cannot be met by repressive police action" or "quieted by token moves or talk." These words took on even greater urgency a few hours later in Jackson, Mississippi, where the NAACP leader Medgar Evers was gunned down and killed by a sniper.

Kennedy followed up his inspiring address by introducing a comprehensive civil rights bill in Congress. It aimed mainly at facilitating school desegregation and opening up public accommodations, such as restaurants and hotels, on an equal basis to Black customers. Fueled by moral outrage, the measure was nonetheless tempered by political caution. The administration refused to press for a provision that would create a commission to guarantee equal employment opportunities for minorities, calculating instead that it would make passage of the bill even more difficult against southern congressional opposition. However, this did not stop civil rights supporters in the legislature from adding this proposal to the bill.

The civil rights forces sought to keep the fires of Kennedy's moral fervor lit by raising the political pressure. A. Philip Randolph now led the massive march on Washington he had first proposed on the eve of World War II. With the NAACP, SCLC, SNCC, and CORE among others behind him, Randolph called on Blacks and whites to rally at the nation's capital for jobs and freedom and, more immediately, to express support for the administration's pending civil rights bill. At first, Kennedy urged Black leaders not to hold the march for fear of creating "an atmosphere of intimidation" that would scare off uncommitted lawmakers whose votes were needed to pass the bill. King brushed these objections aside by reminding the president that a well-disciplined, nonviolent rally would mobilize "support in parts of the country which don't know the problems first hand." Convinced by the planners of their peaceful intentions and willingness to refrain from disrupting government business, Kennedy swung his approval behind the march.

The August 28 rally attracted nearly a quarter of a million people and a good deal of favorable publicity. In a dignified manner it spotlighted the interracial vision of brotherhood that had characterized the early years of the civil rights struggle and found voice in the stirring words of King, who recited his dream that "all God's children, black men and white men, Jews and Gentiles, Protestants and Catholics, will be able to join hands and sing in the words of that old Negro spiritual, 'Free at last! Free at last! Thank God almighty, we are free at last.'"

Once again, rhetoric alone, no matter how well meaning, proved insufficient to secure passage of civil rights legislation. The bill was still stalled in the House of Representatives when Kennedy was assassinated on November 22, 1963. A nation's grief could not immediately break the legislative logjam, even as a memorial to the slain president. It took some eight months of painstaking efforts in Congress before a bipartisan coalition of Democrats and Republicans finally overcame southern opposition. On July 2, 1964, the most far-reaching civil rights statute since Reconstruction went into effect. It expanded the authority of the federal government to challenge school segregation as well as discrimination in public accommodations and employment. To enforce its provisions, the act set up the Equal Employment Opportunity Commission, established the Community Relations Service, and empowered Washington to cut off federal funds to state and local agencies that practiced racial bias.

Though there were pockets of resistance to it, within a relatively short time Jim Crow signs and barriers were removed from public facilities in the South. Progress in desegregating public schools continued slowly, though the law empowered the federal government to cut off funds from school districts that defied court orders to open their doors to Black students. It would take another four years for the Supreme Court to announce once and for all, in *Green v. County School Board* (1968), that further delay was not constitutionally permissible.

PRESIDENT LYNDON B. JOHNSON
AND FREEDOM SUMMER

The movement's legislative agenda received a big boost when Lyndon Baines Johnson entered the White House upon Kennedy's death. The Texan had undergone a stunning transformation with respect to civil rights, from a congressman who had opposed the Truman administration's civil rights program to a vice president who embraced the civil rights movement as a moral and political necessity. Not only was support for racial equality the right thing to do in principle, but it also helped advance Johnson's ambitions to rise to the presidency, recruit enfranchised southern Black voters to the Democratic Party, and give his native South an opportunity to put the corrosive racial issue behind it. Consequently, President Johnson displayed a passion for civil rights advancement that exceeded Kennedy's. A legislative wizard in his days in Congress, Johnson played a large part in engineering passage of the landmark 1964 law.

Besides enactment of this important piece of legislation, Johnson influenced the course of the civil rights movement in other significant ways. In the summer of 1964 civil rights activists in Mississippi launched a campaign to spotlight attention on the state with the lowest percentage of Black registered voters. Organized by the collaborative Council of Federated Organizations (COFO), with SNCC, CORE, and the NAACP in the lead, Freedom Summer brought some six hundred to seven hundred northern white student volunteers into the state, mainly from affluent families and prestigious universities, to set up citizenship training workshops and encourage Blacks to register to vote. COFO's designers had more than the right to vote in mind and sought to provide Black youngsters with educational opportunities that segregation in the Magnolia State had denied them. As a result, about twenty-five hundred students, some of whom were adults, attended freedom schools to improve their literacy and mathematical skills, while at the same time they studied Black history and the civil rights movement to give them a sense of pride in their heritage.

COFO fully expected these heightened activities to lead to white resistance, and given the history of the state, they understood that violence, even killings, might result. Murders of Blacks usually went unpunished and even unnoticed in the South, but the architects of Freedom Summer recognized that similar violence against some of America's best and brightest white youths would attract intense national attention.

The brutal murder of three civil rights workers, one Black and two white, in the first days of Freedom Summer, helped accomplish this. The Justice Department had insisted that it could not provide personal protection for civil rights staff and volunteers, nor could the FBI do more than take notes when racial incidents were reported. Yet the national outrage at the slayings of James Chaney, Michael Schwerner, and Andrew Goodman moved Johnson to direct the FBI to make a concerted effort to bring the perpetrators to justice. As a result, the bureau cracked the case and succeeded in infiltrating and severely damaging the Ku Klux Klan, which was behind the killings.

Still, the president fell short in satisfying civil rights activists in other areas. Out of the voter registration drives of the 1964 summer emerged in the Mississippi Freedom Democratic Party (MFDP). Excluded by the regular white Democratic Party in the state from choosing presidential delegates to attend the 1964 Democratic National Convention in Atlantic City, New Jersey, Blacks and their white allies formed the MFDP to challenge the white delegation's credentials. The insurgents marshaled evidence of how Blacks had been customarily denied the right to vote by state Democratic party officials and refused entrance into Democratic Party deliberations.

However, Johnson had his own agenda. He fashioned a compromise that gave the Freedom Democrats token recognition but allowed his few loyal white supporters to retain their seats in the contested delegation. In contrast, most of the Mississippi regulars refused to support the president and bolted from the convention. Trying to minimize potential defections from white Democrats around the rest of the South, the president had his spokesmen at the convention offer the MFDP two at-large seats but not control over the Mississippi delegation. Promises to reform party rules to prevent racial bias in the future did not assuage the Freedom Democrats, who chose to reject the bargain as a sellout. Recalling the hardships they had endured, MFDP delegate Fannie Lou Hamer, a sharecropper who had been evicted from her home for trying to register, complained, "We didn't come all this way for no two seats." Such criticism did not cause Johnson to budge, and he continued to seek liberal alternatives to what he increasingly regarded as misguided demands from Black radicals.

SELMA AND THE 1965 VOTING RIGHTS ACT

Protests in Selma, Alabama, gave Johnson a fresh opportunity to exert his influence and steer the civil rights movement along "acceptable" paths. Beginning in January 1965, the SCLC had mounted demonstrations to protest continued denial of the right to vote for Blacks. As in Birmingham, King picked a place designed to showcase white resistance and prod the federal government into combating it. On March 7, with television cameras recording their actions, civil rights marchers set out from Selma and headed for the state capital in Montgomery to highlight their grievances. Before they could get very far out of town, state and local police violently attacked them, forcing their bloody retreat. Undaunted, King, who had missed the previous demonstration, scheduled another march for a few days later; however, he agreed to postpone it after the state got a federal court order restraining the fifty-mile trek. The delay proved temporary, and in a few weeks, King and the marchers set out again for Montgomery. In this instance, President Johnson furnished them with military protection after Governor George Wallace refused to do so. The three-month campaign had already resulted in the killing of two protesters, Jimmie Lee Jackson and James Reeb, one Black and the other white. In lending federal assistance, Johnson sought to deter further bloodshed. The civil rights participants reached their final destination, but even the soldiers' presence could not prevent the shooting death of a white female volunteer from Detroit, Viola Liuzzo, on the last day of the pilgrimage.

Johnson helped steer the outcome in another important way. Even before the Selma campaign had begun, the president instructed the Justice Department to prepare proposals to extend the right to vote in the upcoming legislative session. The chief executive preferred the ballot as the method for achieving social change. He contended that once southern Blacks exercised the franchise "many other breakthroughs would follow and they would follow as a consequence of the Black man's own legitimate power as an American, not as a gift from the white man." During the course of the struggle in mid-March, the chief executive went on national television to deliver an address on behalf of Black voting rights, which was every bit as stirring as the one Kennedy gave before introducing the civil rights bill in 1963. Johnson announced his intention of presenting a voting rights measure to Congress and declared that he would tolerate "no delay, no hesitation, no compromise." He followed through swiftly in introducing his recommendation largely because the Justice Department had been preparing one since early in the year.

Although demonstrations in Selma did not create the voting rights bill, they sped up its timetable and ensured that it would contain provisions strong enough to accomplish at long last the goal of enfranchisement. That it did. The Voting Rights Act of 1965 passed Congress in record time and went into effect on August 6, only a few months after it reached the legislature. The law contained several features meant to shift enforcement away from time-consuming litigation in the courts. It covered the southern states in which African Americans had experienced the greatest difficulty in voting: Alabama, Georgia, Louisiana, Mississippi, North Carolina, South Carolina, and Virginia. To avoid further delay, it suspended the use of literacy tests and required the states to clear any future voting changes with the Justice Department before implementing them. It also instructed the Justice Department to challenge the constitutionality of the poll tax in the courts, which it successfully did the following year. For good measure, the statute allowed the attorney general to send federal registrars to enroll Blacks in counties that proved unwilling to comply. With the federal government as a watchdog, by 1969, the majority of southern Blacks were on the voting rolls, and in a remarkable turnabout, approximately 55 percent of eligible Blacks had gained the vote in Mississippi.

The Voting Rights Act marked a watershed in the Black freedom struggle. The Selma to Montgomery March, which hastened passage of the law, brought to a climax the succession of massive demonstrations aimed at pressuring the national government to legislate an end to racial segregation and disfranchisement in the South. Though rallies and protests continued in the years to come, the extension of the right to vote gave African Americans fresh incentive to address their grievances chiefly at the ballot box. More and more, southern Blacks turned their efforts to organizing campaigns to elect African American candidates to public office. In 1964, fewer than twenty-five Black elected officials governed in the South, but by 1970, the number climbed to over seven hundred. Within another decade, Black mayors sat in city halls in Atlanta, Birmingham, and New Orleans, and Black congressmen represented districts in Tennessee, Texas, and Georgia.

BLACK POWER

Following pathbreaking legislative achievements in 1964 and 1965, the movement splintered in several different directions. The NAACP maintained its faith in the traditional goal of integration and the tactics of lobbying Congress and filing litigation in the courts to accomplish it. This association was joined by the National Urban League (NUL). Formed two years after the NAACP in 1911, the NUL engaged in a variety of social service activities to assist African Americans and participated in civil rights efforts to combat racial bias in public and private employment. The two oldest civil rights organizations maintained a close relationship with President Johnson and worked with his administration to enforce the laws that had been recently placed on the books and joined with him to secure still another statute, in 1968, to combat segregation in housing.

On the opposite end of the movement, militant groups such as SNCC and CORE rejected integration and nonviolence and espoused instead racial nationalism and armed self-defense. In 1966, Stokely Carmichael, chairman of SNCC, voiced the battle cry of "Black power," which emphasized racial pride and advocated Black political and economic development free from white interference. "The only way we gonna stop them white men from whippin' us," Carmichael urged a rally in Mississippi, "is to take over. We been saying freedom for six years and we ain't got nothin'. What we gonna start saying is Black Power." SNCC and CORE then broke with the Johnson administration. They denounced white liberals for treating Blacks in a paternalistic manner, pointing to the president's determination to compromise the MFDP's position at the Democratic National Convention in 1964.

The SCLC attempted to occupy the middle ground between these contending factions. King did not approve of the term "Black power," because he considered it too harsh and disliked its antiwhite connotations. Nevertheless, he believed that militants made good sense in advocating racial pride and building up political and economic power in Black communities. However, he did not think that a healthy Black consciousness required excluding white liberals from the struggle for racial justice. Nor did it depend on discarding nonviolence as a philosophy. Like the NAACP and NUL, he attempted to cooperate with the Johnson administration to push it further in the direction of dismantling the remaining barriers to equality, especially with respect to the higher incidence of poverty and unemployment among Blacks than whites. But unlike the other moderates, the SCLC continued to mobilize Blacks to confront racism in the streets. King extended this to the North, where in 1966 he led marches against slum conditions and housing discrimination in Chicago.

PRESIDENT JOHNSON PUSHES RACIAL MODERATION

As in the past, the federal government greatly influenced the direction of the freedom struggle. By temperament and political orientation, Johnson sided with the moderates. In tandem with the NAACP, in 1966, he proposed legislation aimed at combating housing discrimination. After two years of sustained effort, the Johnson administration and its allies persuaded Congress to enact a fair housing law. In addition, the measure armed the Justice Department with increased power to protect the constitutional rights of civil rights workers, a long-standing objective of the movement. In throwing his support behind such legislation, Johnson hoped to reinforce the kind of moderate leaders he favored while undermining the position of radicals in the movement.

He did so again in Mississippi. The president had already shown his considerable influence in determining the outcome of the MFDP convention challenge in 1964. In subsequent years, Johnson boosted the efforts of a rival faction to the MFDP to win recognition as the legitimate party organization representing the Magnolia State. He gave his stamp of approval to the "loyalist" group dominated by the NAACP, moderate whites, and labor unions over the SNCC-backed MFDP. In effect, Johnson guaranteed that the brand of biracial electoral politics favored by the loyalists prevailed over the Freedom Democrat version that increasingly embraced Black power.

The president also undercut SNCC and MFDP in another critical way. The Child Development Group of Mississippi (CDGM) had grown out of the movement's organizing campaigns against disfranchisement and poverty in the state. Starting in 1965, CDGM ran early education classes under the Head Start program funded by Johnson's War on Poverty. Mississippi's white political leaders, especially Senator John Stennis, a segregationist and powerful figure in Washington, opposed the group and threatened to get Congress to cut off its funds. To Stennis, CDGM posed a threat because it was allied with the most radical civil rights organizations in the state, and he considered the organization a front for Black power advocates. Needing Stennis's support to help fund his domestic spending programs as well as the escalating war in Vietnam, Johnson once again struck a bargain. CDGM remained alive, though with inadequate funding, while the Johnson administration funneled antipoverty money to a moderate group of whites and Blacks, Mississippi Action for Progress, more supportive of interracial cooperation and political pragmatism. The outcome of the CDGM controversy produced the same effect as did the handling of the MFDP–Loyalist Democrat battle in the electoral arena. From Washington, the Johnson administration helped determine which groups of Blacks and whites at the local level gained a share of valuable federal resources, thus shaping the course of racial advancement.

RACE RIOTS

Despite his considerable power, the president could not exert total control over a struggle as dynamic and independent as the freedom movement. The riots that swept through the urban ghettos demonstrated this. Starting in 1964 and reaching their peak four years later, these violent insurrections reflected the deep frustrations of African Americans, mainly in the North, for whom civil rights battles in the South had no tangible impact. Black northerners did not need the federal government to grant them the right to vote or access to public facilities on an unsegregated basis; rather, they lacked political power, found themselves mired in poverty, and encountered excessive force from police patrols in their neighborhoods. The Johnson administration could not prevent eruptions from disgruntled residents of Black communities, but at least it did try to open up lines of communication with leaders in these troubled areas. In the end, however, presidential advisers grudgingly admitted that "a lot of this is essentially uncontrollable. It will happen no matter what the federal government does."

Characteristically, Johnson steered a moderate course in dealing with these urban rebellions. He moved between denouncing the rioters and expressing concern for the continuing plight of Blacks. Though highly suspicious about the role played by Black power firebrands such as Stokely Carmichael in fomenting the outbursts, he exercised restraint in agreeing not to prosecute them for allegedly inciting riots. In 1967, the chief executive sent federal troops to Detroit and Newark to restore law and order, much as he and other presidents had acted to quell racial disturbances in Arkansas, Alabama, and Mississippi. He appointed the National Advisory Commission on Civil Disorders, the Kerner Commission, to investigate the problem. In 1968, the commission issued a stinging report blaming white racism as the root cause of rioting and recommended massive federal spending to improve conditions in Black ghettos. However, the president ignored the agency's findings. Johnson's response betrayed more than a bit of personal pique. The miffed president believed that Blacks had not shown him proper gratitude for all he had done to combat racism.

FEDERAL REPRESSION

By 1968, Johnson had effectively parted company from militants in the civil rights alliance. The president's role in escalation of the Vietnam War severed the remaining connections between the national administration and its former allies. SNCC and CORE were among the earliest critics of the president's policies toward Southeast Asia, and after 1965 their representatives had no access to the White House. For several years doubts had been building in King concerning the war, which he had come to see as an evil manifestation of colonialism and racism, but he had kept relatively silent in order not to jeopardize the legislative goals of the civil rights movement. In early 1967, when he could no longer stay quiet and publicly attacked the president's Vietnam policy, King too lost whatever remaining influence he had with the Johnson administration. These defections left Black moderates, who remained loyal to Johnson on the war, in command of the federal civil rights agenda.

Johnson's break with King and the radicals reflected the sinister side of the federal government's relationship with the civil rights movement. Beginning in the Kennedy administration, the White House had authorized the FBI to wiretap King and the SCLC. After his frustrating campaign in Albany, Georgia, King had criticized the bureau for being too cozy with local police and failing to protect the demonstrators. FBI director J. Edgar Hoover, who called King "the most notorious liar in America," warned President Kennedy that the civil rights leader was under Communist influence. He pressured the administration for authority to monitor the activities of the Reverend King, to which it consented partly to prove that the FBI director was wrong in his suspicions. Surveillance continued into the Johnson regime, and as King became more critical of the war and the president, the bureau stepped up its attempts to discredit him by leaking lurid information about sexual indiscretions in his personal life, which it picked up through secretly placed microphones. President Johnson was no stranger to this kind of eavesdropping. Back in 1964, he had instructed the FBI to spy on MFDP members and their allies attending the Democratic National Convention so that he could keep track of their activities as he hammered together the compromise on seating delegates.

Such activities had a debilitating effect on King, but they had a more devastating effect on the most radical sector of the Black freedom movement. As SNCC embraced Black power and its leaders adopted revolutionary rhetoric, the organization became a target of heightened FBI oversight and counterintelligence operations. Having infiltrated and destroyed the Communist Party and the Mississippi Ku Klux Klan, the FBI now aimed to bring down Black leaders it considered a threat. COINTELPRO, as the surveillance program was called, sanctioned attempts not just to watch designated individuals but to disrupt their activities and those of their groups. Hoover's agents sowed the seeds of discord within Black organizations by spreading rumors and planting suspicions that tore groups apart. The bureau worked closely with local law enforcement agencies and supplied information that led to deadly shoot-outs between police and the objects of their surveillance. In one notorious incident, in December 1969, the Chicago police, tipped off by a paid FBI informer within the Black Panthers, raided the group's headquarters and killed two of its leaders, Fred Hampton and Mark Clark. The police claimed they had been ambushed, but the inhabitants had been asleep when the assault began. A subsequent investigation cast serious doubt concerning the police account, finding that while one shot had been fired from within the building, eighty-three bullets had entered the apartment.

In this way, organizations such as SNCC and the Black Panther Party for Self Defense, two of the most militant groups of the period, felt the sting of federal power. Though these groups also suffered from problems of their own making, there is no doubt that they could not withstand Hoover's brand of federal harassment. By the mid-1970s,

SNCC had ceased functioning and the Panthers had been hounded into exhaustion and exile, sent to jail, or buried in their graves.

LEGACY OF THE CIVIL RIGHTS MOVEMENT AND AFFIRMATIVE ACTION

Indeed, by the end of the 1960s the civil rights movement, as it had existed for over two decades, had come to a conclusion. Martin Luther King fell to an assassin's bullet in April 1968, and though the SCLC remained in operation, it never recovered from the loss of its charismatic head. With SNCC and CORE on the decline, this left the NAACP and the NUL as the major survivors of the old civil rights alliance. The moderates had scored three major legislative victories and won numerous battles in the courts to enforce desegregation and disfranchisement. However, even moderation was not enough to sustain the struggle at the national level once conservatives captured the White House beginning with Richard Nixon in 1968. For the most part, the civil rights groups that remained in existence sought to preserve the legislative and judicial victories they had obtained and see that they were properly enforced. However, more than a quarter of a century later, the legacy of the Black freedom struggle has come under attack.

The program targeted for the most criticism has been affirmative action. During the 1960s, the federal government recognized that African Americans needed more than equality as a legal principle; they required policies that would result in equality in practice. Since race had been used by whites for centuries to victimize them, Blacks would not be able to overcome the pervasive effects of past discrimination without the legal and political system taking race into account, this time in their favor. In a speech at Howard University in June 1965, President Johnson eloquently defended the proposition that affirmative steps must be taken to close the economic gap between whites and Blacks to achieve "equality as a fact." To this end, affirmative action was considered as a reasonable means of compensating African Americans for past wrongs and the most effective way of obtaining significant results in their lifetime.

Although supported by civil rights leaders, affirmative action plans were shaped mainly by federal officials. Johnson backed up his words by signing an executive order requiring federal vendors actively to recruit and hire qualified minority job seekers. In 1968, the Department of Labor instructed major contractors to adopt proposals that set timetables to achieve specific goals guaranteeing "full and equal employment opportunity" for minorities. The Equal Employment Opportunity Commission, established by Congress in the 1964 Civil Rights Act, shaped the pattern of affirmative action enforcement by judging discrimination not on the basis of intentional bias against a particular individual but by looking at the effects on the aggrieved group. In this way, federal bureaucrats used statistics to prove racial and sexual discrimination when African Americans and women were not proportionately represented in the workplace. This approach also extended to admission to colleges and universities and election to public office. Concerning the latter, Justice Department officials challenged election systems that limited the chance of Black voters to choose members of their own race to represent them. Consequently, they measured discrimination by the continuing gap between the percentage of Black officeholders and the proportion of Blacks in the population.

Affirmative action generated a great deal of opposition, mainly from whites. Critics denounced it as a form of preferential treatment for Blacks and thereby reverse discrimination against whites. They rejected the idea that African Americans were entitled to special consideration as members of a racial group and argued that allegations of bias must be proven only against individuals committing the offense. Defining discrimination according to a standard of proportional representation, they contended, violated norms of fair play required in a color-blind society in which merit, not skin color, should govern.

Since the mid-1970s, these arguments have gained momentum. The federal judiciary, including the Supreme Court, which had done so much to expand the concept of equality, began chipping away at affirmative action plans, leaving them with very limited scope for enforcement. States such as Texas and California have virtually abolished affirmative action as public policy and received approval from the federal courts. Thus, without vigorous support from the federal government, this program designed to achieve genuine equality is withering away.

THE ROLE OF THE NATIONAL GOVERNMENT

Throughout the history of the civil rights struggle, the national state played a key role in determining its outcome. Beginning with the Tru-

man administration, the president and his allies in Congress set the legis-
lative agenda that would guide lawmakers for the next three decades.
Truman's Committee on Civil Rights sketched out the plans that were
used to attack segregation and disfranchisement, culminating in the 1964
Civil Rights Act and the 1965 Voting Rights Act. Starting with *Smith v.
Allwright* in 1944 and *Brown v. Board of Education* a decade later, the
Supreme Court placed constitutional law on the side of those seeking to
extend the right to vote and topple Jim Crow. Presidents Eisenhower,
Kennedy, and Johnson flexed their federal muscles at key moments to
smash southern white resistance to court-ordered desegregation.

At the same time, it must be recognized that Washington usually
acted cautiously and incrementally. The White House and Congress
rarely moved ahead of public opinion, and when the Supreme Court
did get out in front it could not enforce its rulings without assistance
from the chief executive and lawmakers. Even the most activist presidents, Kennedy and Johnson, viewed their options more narrowly than
civil rights proponents wished. The occupants of the White House believed that the constitutional boundaries of the federal system restricted
them from intervening to protect civil rights workers in the South,
thereby exposing these freedom fighters to increased harm and causing
bitterness and disillusionment. Too often presidents weighed the political
ramifications of their actions more than the moral dimensions of the
struggle against racism, especially with powerful southern Democrats in
key positions in Congress. As a result, federal officials affected the strategy of civil rights proponents by encouraging them to provoke crises in
order to force action from Washington.

Furthermore, the most sympathetic resident of the Oval Office,
Lyndon Johnson, showed how a president could directly affect the
course of the civil rights struggle by using his power to forge compro-
mises and allocate resources to favored allies. Johnson helped augment
the power of moderates within the movement just as more radical factions sought to reshape the freedom struggle. Militant radicals found it
difficult to survive, not only without federal support but in the face of
federal opposition, as the target of surveillance and intimidation.

The case to be made for the importance of the federal government
is strengthened by looking at the post–civil rights era. Though the national civil rights coalition collapsed with the end of the 1960s, the federal government continued to enforce the laws against segregation and

disfranchisement that had so recently been placed on the books. Indeed, bureaucrats in the Justice Department's Civil Rights Division and agencies such as the Equal Employment Opportunity Commission adopted novel affirmative action approaches to advance the fortunes of African Americans economically and politically. However, as opponents of these policies captured the White House, Congress, and the Supreme Court in the 1980s and 1990s, they have stalled and begun to reverse these hard-earned accomplishments. Having defeated public segregation and acquired the right to vote during the Second Reconstruction, African Americans remember the lesson of the First Reconstruction after the Civil War. Withdrawal by the federal government has left their constitutional protections vulnerable to attack.

Of course, Washington alone cannot supply all the answers. As was the case during the civil rights movement, African Americans must organize to achieve their own freedom. The federal government made racial reform possible, but Blacks in the South made it necessary. Had they not mobilized their neighbors, opened their churches to stage protests and sustain the spirits of the demonstrators, and rallied the faithful to provoke a response from the federal government, far less progress would have been made. Thus, the real heroes of the civil rights struggle were the Black foot soldiers and their white allies who directly put their lives on the line in the face of often overwhelming odds against them. Federal officials were not heroes, for they usually calculated the political consequences of their actions too closely and raised their voices too ambiguously. Yet if not heroes, they proved essential for allowing the truly courageous to succeed.

THE FORGOTTEN LEGACY OF MARTIN LUTHER KING, JR.

Dr. King has an ironic relationship with the history of the civil rights movement. On the one hand, he embodies the values of integration, brotherhood, nonviolence, and faith in the power of redemption. The idealism expressed in the language of King's dream of racial harmony articulated at the march on Washington in 1963 remains the basis of the annual celebration of the civil rights leader's birthday as a national holiday. On the other hand, over the past two decades King has not fared well with historians who regard him as merely one among many leaders of the movement and not necessarily the most important one. In this view, the main force behind the struggle came not from Dr. King but from the Black women and men who organized their individual communities to obtain their freedom.

This alternative vision has gained ascendancy with many young people today born after Dr. King became a national icon. They gravitate toward figures like Malcolm X, Huey Newton and his comrades in the Black Panther Party, and Robert F. Williams, an early exponent of armed self-defense. These freedom fighters capture the imagination of young people because they sharply denounced white oppressors and asserted fierce pride in their Black heritage. By contrast, King appears tame, too willing to turn the other cheek, and not Black or revolutionary enough. The fact that he succeeded in helping to dismantle Jim Crow and extend the ballot through national legislation only reinforces the view that King "sold out" to the system to get what he wanted.

Largely forgotten or conveniently ignored, King was a genuine revolutionary—one of his aides called him the "most radical cat of the twentieth century"—who sought to reconstruct the lives not only of African Americans but of all Americans. He valued integration as a means of achieving "a beloved community"; however, he understood that fallible human beings, including those who governed the United States, responded more to demonstrations of power than to sermons about love and Christian duty.

Although using the term "passive resistance," King placed emphasis on the noun rather than the adjective. Whatever King may have called it, he and his supporters engaged in active not passive resistance, experiencing dangerous confrontations not meek encounters. For example, during voting rights demonstrations in Selma, Alabama in 1965, King's aide, the Reverend C. T. Vivian, climbed the Dallas County Courthouse steps and lectured Sheriff Jim Clark about his Nazi-like treatment of protesters. Clark promptly slugged his tormentor, vividly proving that nonviolent resistance was hardly passive.

King's commitment to nonviolence as a basic principle of struggle proved revolutionary. The militant Black leader H. Rap Brown of SNCC asserted, "violence is as American as cherry pie," but King and his followers went against the grain. They advocated *disciplined* nonviolence, which required a radical transformation of individual behavior in a society that routinely encouraged armed self-defense and turned might into right. Dr. King and his associates recognized that nonviolence did not come easily or instinctively and conducted intensive training sessions and workshops to overcome the inclination to fight back in the face of attack. Yet King did not disparage the right of self-defense. He believed that what might work for individuals under assault would fail as a political strategy for a minority group seeking freedom and requiring support from white allies to win it.

In pursuing his goals, Dr. King furnished a new model of Black manhood. Given the long history of violence against Black men and the attempted evisceration of their manhood to preserve white male supremacy, it is not surprising that by the late 1960s appeals to a muscular Black masculinity, identified with Malcolm X, Muhammad Ali, and the Black Panthers, had attracted widespread support among African Americans. Malcolm X had belittled King for preaching a nonviolent philosophy in which men allowed their wives and children to be beaten without fighting back to protect them. King offered an alternative vision of what it meant to be a Black man. For him, self-control in the face of immediate danger provided the ultimate test of courage, and it was no less a sign of masculinity for Black men to demonstrate bravery and measure their self-worth by disciplining themselves to endure suffering in pursuit of the higher cause of social justice. In doing so, they did not show passiveness or cowardice but demonstrated personal strength and heroism. Notwithstanding these views, King was also a product of his times with traditional ideas about women and sexuality. If his version of manhood incorporated common notions about the dependent role of women, he scarcely differed from Malcolm X, Stokely Carmichael, and most male, Black militant critics.

Nor did King's approach to resistance, which eschewed violence and called for racial nationalism, undermine respect for Black identity. King rejected the slogan of Black Power as an empty and impolitic phrase when it gained notoriety after 1965, but he did not ridicule the basic concept. The scion of a respected Black family who attended Black public schools and a Black college and who became a pastor in the quintessential Black cultural institution of the church, the Reverend King reflected the richness of the African American experience. He did not favor integration to diminish Black self-esteem, but saw it as a way for African Americans to contribute to and gain from the ethnic diversity that ideally united the American people. In his first public speech at the outset of the Montgomery bus boycott in 1955, Dr. King emphasized Black pride: "When the history books are written in future generations, the historians will have to pause and say 'There lived a great people—a Black people—who injected new meaning and dignity into the veins of civilization.'"

To a greater extent than usually recognized, throughout his lifetime King was branded a radical. Even during the late 1950s and early 1960s, when King's public language could be considered most moderate, politicians and the media attacked him as a public nuisance. Both in print and on television, commentators criticized King for promoting civil disobedience, which they interpreted as disrespect for law and order and encouraging criminal behavior in the name of a higher morality. His public approval fluctuated according to his tactics and how much violence they occasioned. Sheriff Laurie Pritchett in Albany, Georgia outfoxed King and won over the national media by appearing to operate with restraint in dealing with demonstrators, whereas "Bull" Connor and Jim Clark played into King's hands with excessive use of force in curtailing protests. Nevertheless, while supporting civil rights legislation in 1964 and 1965, most whites believed that King's tactics had gone too far in provoking bloodshed and wanted his protests to slow down.

By the time of King's assassination in April 1968, the civil rights leader had lost even more public approval and support from President Lyndon Johnson, and he labored under constant surveillance by the FBI. Besides continuing active resistance in Chicago, Memphis, and with plans for a poor peoples' crusade in Washington, D.C., King drew the ire of many white and Black civil rights allies by vigorously denouncing the Vietnam War and American imperialism as well as condemning materialism and capitalism. A year before his death in April 1967, King declared that unless the United States found an end to the war in Vietnam "we shall surely be dragged down the long dark and shameful corridors of time reserved for those who possess power without compassion, might without morality, and strength without sight." His complaint went beyond the conflict in Vietnam, and he asserted that "our only hope today lies in our ability to recapture the revolutionary spirit and go out into a sometimes hostile world declaring eternal hostility to poverty, racism, and militarism." In voicing these views, Dr. King had become the dissident most feared by the government when he died.

As a national leader King became a convenient target for Black and white critics attacking the shortcomings of the civil rights movement. Yet even more than a national figure, King functioned as what the sociologist Belinda Robnett termed a "bridge leader." Refusing to forget the distinct Christian voices of southern Blacks, he continued to work in communities that beckoned him to jumpstart their protests. A quasi ambassador of Black America, he fought tirelessly to bring federal power on the side of struggling Black communities. Grassroots organizing proved essential to laying the groundwork and solidifying the movement, but so too did the presence of Martin Luther King, Jr., a charismatic leader who connected national and local forces. One may disparage his style of leadership, but the fact that no one has arrived on the scene to replace him these past forty years testifies to his significance. To the extent that the civil rights movement spawned many leaders, King stood as the first among equals. In the words of Stokely Carmichael, who both criticized and admired him, King was "the one man of our race that this country's older generation, the militants, and the revolutionaries and the masses of Black people would still listen to." A successor to Dr. King has not appeared, but his forgotten legacy can provide renewed inspiration for peace, justice, and equality at home and abroad.

Documents

1

EXCERPT FROM
TO SECURE THESE RIGHTS:
THE REPORT OF THE PRESIDENT'S
COMMITTEE ON CIVIL RIGHTS (1947)

Sadie T. Alexander, James B. Carey, John S. Dickey,
Morris L. Ernst, Roland B. Gittelsohn, Frank P. Graham,
Francis J. Haas, Charles Luckman, Francis P. Matthews,
Franklin D. Roosevelt, Jr., Henry Knox Sherrill, Boris Shishkin,
Dorothy Tilly, Channing Tobias, Charles E. Wilson, *Chairman*

A PROGRAM OF ACTION:
THE COMMITTEE'S RECOMMENDATIONS

The Time Is Now

Twice before in American history the nation has found it necessary to review the state of its civil rights. The first time was during the 15 years between 1776 and 1791, from the drafting of the Declaration of Independence through the Articles of Confederation experiment to the writing of the Constitution and the Bill of Rights. It was then that the distinctively American heritage was finally distilled from earlier views of liberty. The second time was when the Union was temporarily sundered over the question of whether it could exist "half-slave" and "half-free."

It is our profound conviction that we have come to a time for a third re-examination of the situation, and a sustained drive ahead. Our reasons for believing this are those of conscience, of self-interest, and of survival in a threatening world. Or to put it another way, we have a moral reason, an economic reason, and an international reason for believing that the time for action is now.

THE MORAL REASON

We have considered the American heritage of freedom at some length. We need no further justification for a broad and immediate program than the need to reaffirm our faith in the traditional American morality. The pervasive gap between our aims and what we actually do is creating a kind of moral dry rot which eats away at the emotional and rational basis of democratic beliefs. There are times when the difference between what we preach about civil rights and what we practice is shockingly illustrated by individual outrages. There are times when the whole structure of our ideology is made ridiculous by individual instances. And there are certain continuing, quiet, omnipresent practices which do irreparable damage to our beliefs.

As examples of "moral erosion" there are the consequences of suffrage limitations in the South. The fact that Negroes and many whites have not been allowed to vote in some states has actually sapped the morality underlying universal suffrage. Many men in public and private life do not believe that those who have been kept from voting are capable of self rule. They finally convince themselves that disfranchised people do not really have the right to vote.

Wartime segregation in the armed forces is another instance of how a social pattern may wreak moral havoc. Practically all white officers and enlisted men in all branches of service saw Negro military personnel performing only the most menial functions. They saw Negroes recruited for the common defense treated as men apart and distinct from themselves. As a result, men who might otherwise have maintained the equalitarian morality of their forebears were given reason to look down on their fellow citizens. This has been sharply illustrated by the Army study discussed previously, in which white servicemen expressed great surprise at the excellent performance of Negroes who joined them in the firing line. Even now, very few people know of the successful experiment with integrated combat units. Yet it is important in explaining why some Negro troops did not do well; it is proof that equal treatment can produce equal performance.

Thousands upon thousands of small, unseen incidents reinforce the impact of headlined violations like lynchings, and broad social patterns like segregation and inequality of treatment. There is, for example, the matter of "fair play." As part of its training for democratic life, our youth is constantly told to "play fair," to abide by "the rules of the game," and to be "good sports." Yet, how many boys and girls in our country experience such things as Washington's annual marble tournament? Because of the prevailing pattern of segregation, established as a model for youth in the schools and recreation systems, separate tournaments are held for Negro and white boys. Parallel elimination contests are sponsored until only two victors remain. Without a contest between them, the white boy is automatically designated as the local champion and sent to the national tournament, while the Negro lad is relegated to the position of runner-up. What child can achieve any real understanding of fair play, or sportsmanship, of the rules of the game, after he has personally experienced such an example of inequality?

It is impossible to decide who suffers the greatest moral damage from our civil rights transgressions, because all of us are hurt. That is certainly true of those who are victimized. Their belief in the basic truth of the American promise is undermined. But they do have the realization, galling as it sometimes is, of being morally in the right. The damage to those who are responsible for these violations of our moral standards may well be greater. They, too, have been reared to honor the command of "free and equal." And all of us must share in the shame at the growth of hypocrisies like the "automatic" marble champion. All of us must endure the cynicism about democratic values which our failures breed.

The United States can no longer countenance these burdens on its common conscience, these inroads on its moral fiber.

THE ECONOMIC REASON

One of the principal economic problems facing us and the rest of the world is achieving maximum production and continued prosperity. The loss of a huge, potential market for goods is a direct result of the economic discrimination which is practiced against many of our minority groups. A sort of vicious circle is produced. Discrimination depresses the wages and income of minority groups. As a result, their purchasing power is curtailed and markets are reduced. Reduced markets result in reduced production. This cuts down employment, which of course means lower wages and still fewer job opportunities. Rising fear, prejudice, and insecurity aggravate the very discrimination in employment which sets the vicious circle in motion.

Minority groups are not the sole victims of this economic waste; its impact is inevitably felt by the entire population. Eric Johnston, when President of the United States Chamber of Commerce, made this point with vividness and clarity:

> The withholding of jobs and business opportunities from some people does not make more jobs and business opportunities for others. Such a policy merely tends to drag down the whole economic level. You can't sell an electric refrigerator to a family that can't afford electricity. Perpetuating poverty for some merely guarantees stagnation for all. True economic progress demands that the whole nation move forward at the same time. It demands that all artificial barriers erected by ignorance and intolerance be removed. To put it in the simplest terms, we are all in business together. Intolerance is a species of boycott and any business or job boycott is a cancer in the economic body of the nation. I repeat, intolerance is destructive; prejudice produces no wealth; discrimination is a fool's economy.

Economic discrimination prevents full use of all our resources. During the war, when we were called upon to make an all-out productive effort, we found that we lacked skilled laborers. This shortage might not have been so serious if minorities had not frequently been denied opportunities for training and experience. In the end, it cost large amounts of money and precious time to provide ourselves with trained persons.

Discrimination imposes a direct cost upon our economy through the wasteful duplication of many facilities and services required by the "separate but equal" policy. That the resources of the South are sorely strained by the burden of a double system of schools and other public services has already been indicated. Segregation is also economically wasteful for private business. Public transportation companies must often provide duplicate facilities to serve majority and minority groups separately. Places of public accommodation and recreation reject business when it comes in the form of unwanted persons. Stores reduce their

DISCRIMINATION IN EMPLOYMENT MEANS . . .

FAIR EMPLOYMENT PRACTICES WOULD HELP BRING . . .

LESS PURCHASING POWER

LESS CONSUMER DEMAND

LESS PRODUCTION

. . . AND A LOWER LIVING STANDARD FOR ALL

INEFFICIENT USE OF OUR LABOR FORCE

GREATER PURCHASING POWER

GREATER CONSUMER DEMAND

FULL PRODUCTION

. . . AND A HIGHER LIVING STANDARD FOR ALL

FULL AND EFFICIENT USE OF ALL OUR WORKERS . . .

sales by turning away minority customers. Factories must provide separate locker rooms, pay windows, drinking fountains, and washrooms for the different groups.

Discrimination in wage scales and hiring policies forces a higher proportion of some minority groups onto relief rolls than corresponding segments of the majority. A study by the Federal Emergency Relief Administration during the depression of the Thirties revealed that in every region the percentage of Negro families on relief was far greater than white families:

	Per cent of families on relief, May, 1934	
	Negro	*White*
Northern cities	52.2	13.3
Border state cities	51.8	10.4
Southern cities	33.7	11.4

Similarly, the rates of disease, crime, and fires are disproportionately great in areas which are economically depressed as compared with wealthier areas. Many of the prominent American minorities are confined—by economic discrimination, by law, by restrictive covenants, and by social pressure—to the most dilapidated, undesirable locations. Property in these locations yields a smaller return in taxes, which is seldom sufficient to meet the inordinately high cost of public services in depressed areas. The majority pays a high price in taxes for the low status of minorities.

To the costs of discrimination must be added the expensive investigations, trials, and property losses which result from civil rights violations. In the aggregate, these attain huge proportions. The 1943 Detroit riot alone resulted in the destruction of two million dollars in property.

Finally, the cost of prejudice cannot be computed in terms of markets, production, and expenditures. Perhaps the most expensive results are the least tangible ones. No nation can afford to have its component groups hostile toward one another without feeling the stress. People who live in a state of tension and suspicion cannot use their energy constructively. The frustrations of their restricted existence are translated into aggression against the dominant group. [Gunnar] Myrdal says:

> Not only occasional acts of violence, but most laziness, carelessness,
> unreliability, petty stealing and lying are undoubtedly to be explained

as concealed aggression ★ ★ ★. The truth is that *Negroes generally do not feel they have unqualified moral obligations to white people* ★ ★ ★. The voluntary withdrawal which has intensified the isolation between the two castes is also an expression of Negro protest under cover.

It is not at all surprising that a people relegated to second-class citizenship should behave as second-class citizens. This is true, in varying degrees, of all of our minorities. What we have lost in money, production, invention, citizenship, and leadership as the price for damaged, thwarted personalities—these are beyond estimate.

The United States can no longer afford this heavy drain upon its human wealth, its national competence.

THE INTERNATIONAL REASON

Our position in the postwar world is so vital to the future that our smallest actions have far-reaching effects. We have come to know that our own security in a highly interdependent world is inextricably tied to the security and well-being of all people and all countries. Our foreign policy is designed to make the United States an enormous, positive influence for peace and progress throughout the world. We have tried to let nothing, not even extreme political differences between ourselves and foreign nations, stand in the way of this goal. But our domestic civil rights shortcomings are a serious obstacle.

In a letter to the Fair Employment Practice Committee on May 8, 1946, the Honorable Dean Acheson, then Acting Secretary of State, stated that:

> ★ ★ ★ the existence of discrimination against minority groups in this country has an adverse effect upon our relations with other countries. We are reminded over and over by some foreign newspapers and spokesmen, that our treatment of various minorities leaves much to be desired. While sometimes these pronouncements are exaggerated and unjustified, they all too frequently point with accuracy to some form of discrimination because of race, creed, color, or national origin. Frequently we find it next to impossible to formulate a satisfactory answer to our critics in other countries; the gap between the things we stand for in principle and the facts of a particular situation may be

too wide to be bridged. An atmosphere of suspicion and resentment in a country over the way a minority is being treated in the United States is a formidable obstacle to the development of mutual understanding and trust between the two countries. We will have better international relations when these reasons for suspicion and resentment have been removed.

I think it is quite obvious ★ ★ ★ that the existence of discriminations against minority groups in the United States is a handicap in our relations with other countries. The Department of State, therefore, has good reason to hope for the continued and increased effectiveness of public and private efforts to do away with these discriminations.

The people of the United States stem from many lands. Other nations and their citizens are naturally intrigued by what has happened to their American "relatives." Discrimination against, or mistreatment of, any racial, religious or national group in the United States is not only seen as our internal problem. The dignity of a country, a continent, or even a major portion of the world's population, may be outraged by it. A relatively few individuals here may be identified with millions of people elsewhere, and the way in which they are treated may have world-wide repercussions. We have fewer than half a million American Indians; there are 30 million more in the Western Hemisphere. Our Mexican American and Hispano groups are not large; millions in Central and South America consider them kin. We number our citizens of Oriental descent in the hundreds of thousands; their counterparts overseas are numbered in hundreds of millions. Throughout the Pacific, Latin America, Africa, the Near, Middle, and Far East, the treatment which our Negroes receive is taken as a reflection of our attitudes toward all dark-skinned peoples.

In the recent war, citizens of a dozen European nations were happy to meet Smiths, Cartiers, O'Haras, Schultzes, di Salvos, Cohens, and Sklodowskas and all the others in our armies. Each nation could share in our victories because its "sons" had helped win them. How much of this good feeling was dissipated when they found virulent prejudice among some of our troops is impossible to say.

We cannot escape the fact that our civil rights record has been an issue in world politics. The world's press and radio are full of it. This Committee has seen a multitude of samples. We and our friends have been, and are, stressing our achievements. Those with competing philosophies have stressed—and are shamelessly distorting—our shortcomings. They have not only tried to create hostility toward us among specific nations, races, and religious groups. They have tried to prove our democracy an empty fraud, and our nation a consistent oppressor of underprivileged people. This may seem ludicrous to Americans, but it is sufficiently important to worry our friends. The following United Press dispatch from London proves that (*Washington Post*, May 25, 1947):

> Although the Foreign Office reserved comment on recent lynch activities in the Carolinas, British diplomatic circles said privately today that they have played into the hands of Communist propagandists in Europe ★ ★ ★.
>
> Diplomatic circles said the two incidents of mob violence would provide excellent propaganda ammunition for Communist agents who have been decrying America's brand of "freedom" and "democracy."
>
> News of the North Carolina kidnapping was prominently displayed by London papers ★ ★ ★.

The international reason for acting to secure our civil rights now is not to win the approval of our totalitarian critics. We would not expect it if our record were spotless; to them our civil rights record is only a convenient weapon with which to attack us. Certainly we would like to deprive them of that weapon. But we are more concerned with the good opinion of the peoples of the world. Our achievements in building and maintaining a state dedicated to the fundamentals of freedom have already served as a guide for those seeking the best road from chaos to liberty and prosperity. But it is not indelibly written that democracy will encompass the world. We are convinced that our way of life—the free way of life—holds a promise of hope for all people. We have what is perhaps the greatest responsibility ever placed upon a people to keep this promise alive. Only still greater achievements will do it.

The United States is not so strong, the final triumph of the democratic ideal is not so inevitable that we can ignore what the world thinks of us or our record.

DISCUSSION QUESTIONS

1. Which one of the three reasons presented in the report for taking action against racial discrimination do you consider most important? Why?
2. The report refers to a "distinctively American heritage . . . distilled from earlier views of liberty." Hoes does this "heritage" apply to the experience of African Americans?

2

DECLARATION OF
CONSTITUTIONAL PRINCIPLES:
THE SOUTHERN MANIFESTO
(MARCH 12, 1956)

[*The complete text of the manifesto and signers (all Democrats unless otherwise noted)*]

The unwarranted decision of the Supreme Court in the public school cases is now bearing the fruit always produced when men substitute naked power for established law.

The Founding Fathers gave us a Constitution of checks and balances because they realized the inescapable lesson of history that no man or group of men can be safely entrusted with unlimited power. They framed this Constitution with its provisions for change by amendment in order to secure the fundamentals of government against the dangers of temporary popular passion or the personal predilections of public office holders.

We regard the decision of the Supreme Court in the school cases as a clear abuse of judicial power. It climaxes a trend in the federal judiciary undertaking to legislate, in derogation of the authority of Congress, and to encroach upon the reserved rights of the States and the people.

The original Constitution does not mention education. Neither does the Fourteenth Amendment nor any other Amendment. The debates preceding the submission of the Fourteenth Amendment clearly show that there was no intent that it should affect the systems of education maintained by the States.

The very Congress which proposed the Amendment subsequently provided for segregated schools in the District of Columbia.

ESTABLISHED SEGREGATED SCHOOLS

When the Amendment was adopted in 1868, there were 37 States of the Union. Every one of the 26 States that had any substantial racial differences among its people either approved the operation of segregated schools already in existence or subsequently established such schools by action of the same lawmaking body which considered the Fourteenth Amendment.

As admitted by the Supreme Court in the public school case (*Brown v. Board of Education*), the doctrine of separate but equal schools "apparently originated in *Roberts v. City of Boston* . . . (1849), upholding school segregation against attack as being violative of a State constitutional guarantee of equality." This constitutional doctrine began in the North—not in the South, and it was followed not only in Massachusetts, but in Connecticut, New York, Illinois, Indiana, Michigan, Minnesota, New Jersey, Ohio, Pennsylvania and other northern States until they, exercising their rights as States through the constitutional processes of local self-government, changed their school systems.

In the case of *Plessy v. Ferguson* in 1896 the Supreme Court expressly declared that under the Fourteenth Amendment no person was denied any of his rights if the States provided separate but equal public facilities. This decision has been followed in many other cases. It is notable that the Supreme Court, speaking through Chief Justice Taft, a former President of the United States, unanimously declared in 1927 in *Lum v. Rice* that the "separate but equal" principle is ". . . within the discretion of the State in regulating its public schools and does not conflict with the Fourteenth Amendment."

This interpretation, restated time and again, became a part of the life of the people of many of the States and confirmed their habits, customs, traditions and way of life. It is founded on elemental humanity and common sense, for parents should not be deprived by government of the right to direct the lives and education of their own children.

'NO LEGAL BASIS'

Though there has been no constitutional amendment or Act of Congress changing this established legal principle almost a century old, the Supreme Court of the United States, with no legal basis for such action, undertook to exercise their naked judicial power and substituted their personal political and social ideas for the established law of the land.

This unwarranted exercise of power by the Court, contrary to the Constitution, is creating chaos and confusion in the States principally affected. It is destroying the amicable relations between the white and Negro races that have been created through 90 years of patient effort by the good people of both races. It has planted hatred and suspicion where there has been heretofore friendship and understanding.

Without regard to the consent of the governed, outside agitators are threatening immediate and revolutionary changes in our public school systems. If done, this is certain to destroy the system of public education in some of the States.

With the gravest concern for the explosive and dangerous condition created by this decision and inflamed by outside meddlers:

We reaffirm our reliance on the Constitution as the fundamental law of the land.

We decry the Supreme Court's encroachments on rights reserved to the States and to the people, contrary to established law and to the Constitution.

COMMEND MOTIVES

We commend the motives of those States which have declared the intention to resist forced integration by any lawful means.

We appeal to the States and people who are not directly affected by these decisions to consider the constitutional principles involved against the time when they too, on issues vital to them, may be the victims of judicial encroachment.

Even though we constitute a minority in the present Congress, we have full faith that a majority of the American people believe in the dual system of government which has enabled us to achieve our greatness and will in time demand that the reserved rights of the States and of the people be made secure against judicial usurpation.

We pledge ourselves to use all lawful means to bring about a reversal of this decision which is contrary to the Constitution and to prevent the use of force in its implementation.

In this trying period, as we all seek to right this wrong, we appeal to our people not to be provoked by the agitators and troublemakers invading our States and to scrupulously refrain from disorder and lawless acts.

Signed by:

Members of the United States Senate:

Walter F. George (Ga.)
Richard B. Russell (Ga.)
John Stennis (Miss.)
Sam J. Ervin Jr. (N.C.)
Strom Thurmond (S.C.)
Harry F. Byrd (Va.)
A. Willis Robertson (Va.)
John L. McClellan (Ark.)
Allen J. Ellender (La.)
Russell B. Long (La.)

Lister Hill (Ala.)
James O. Eastland (Miss.)
W. Kerr Scott (N.C.)
John Sparkman (Ala.)
Olin D. Johnston (S.C.)
Price Daniel (Texas)
J. W. Fulbright (Ark.)
George A. Smathers (Fla.)
Spessard L. Holland (Fla.)

Members of the United States House of Representatives:

ALABAMA

Frank W. Boykin
George M. Grant
George W. Andrews
Kenneth A. Roberts
Albert Rains

Armistead I. Selden Jr.
Carl Elliott
Robert E. Jones
George Huddleston Jr.

ARKANSAS

E. C. Gathings
Wilbur D. Mills
James W. Trimble

Oren Harris
Brooks Hays
W. F. Norrell

FLORIDA

Charles E. Bennett
Robert L. F. Sikes
William Cramer (R)
A. S. Herlong Jr.

Paul G. Rogers
James A. Haley
D. R. Matthews

GEORGIA

Prince H. Preston
John L. Pilcher
E. L. Forrester
John James Flynt Jr.
James C. Davis

Carl Vinson
Henderson Lanham
Iris F. Blitch
Phil M. Landrum
Paul Brown

LOUISIANA

F. Edward Hebert
Hale Boggs
Edwin E. Willis
Overton Brooks

Otto E. Passman
James H. Morrison
T. Ashton Thompson
George S. Long

MISSISSIPPI

Thomas G. Abernethy
Jamie L. Whitten
Frank E. Smith

John Bell Williams
Arthur Winstead
William M. Colmer

NORTH CAROLINA

Herbert C. Bonner
L. H. Fountain
Graham A. Barden
Carl T. Durham
F. Ertel Carlyle

Hugh O. Alexander
Woodrow W. Jones
George A. Shuford
Charles Raper Jonas (R)

SOUTH CAROLINA

L. Mendel Rivers
John J. Riley
W. J. Bryan Dorn

Robert T. Ashmore
James P. Richards
John L. McMillan

TENNESSEE

James B. Frazier Jr.
Ross Bass
Tom Murray

Jere Cooper
Clifford Davis
Joe L. Evins

TEXAS

Wright Patman
Martin Dies
John Dowdy

Walter Rogers
O. C. Fisher

VIRGINIA

Edward J. Robeson Jr.
Porter Hardy Jr.
J. Vaughan Gary
Watkins M. Abbitt
William M. Tuck

Richard H. Poff (R)
Burr P. Harrison
Howard W. Smith
W. Pat Jennings
Joel T. Broyhill (R)

DISCUSSION QUESTIONS

1. On what legal/constitutional basis does the manifesto defend its position of resistance?
2. Senator Lyndon B. Johnson's name was not among those of the signers. Why not?

3

DWIGHT D. EISENHOWER'S RADIO AND TELEVISION ADDRESS TO THE AMERICAN PEOPLE ON THE SITUATION IN LITTLE ROCK (SEPTEMBER 24, 1957)

Good Evening, My Fellow Citizens:

For a few minutes this evening I want to speak to you about the serious situation that has arisen in Little Rock. To make this talk I have come to the President's office in the White House. I could have spoken from Rhode Island, where I have been staying recently, but I felt that, in speaking from the house of Lincoln, of Jackson and of Wilson, my words would better convey both the sadness I feel in the action I was compelled today to take and the firmness with which I intend to pursue this course until the orders of the Federal Court at Little Rock can be executed without unlawful interference.

In that city, under the leadership of demagogic extremists, disorderly mobs have deliberately prevented the carrying out of proper orders from a Federal Court. Local authorities have not eliminated that violent opposition and, under the law, I yesterday issued a Proclamation calling upon the mob to disperse.

This morning the mob again gathered in front of the Central High School of Little Rock, obviously for the purpose of again preventing the carrying out of the Court's order relating to the admission of Negro children to that school.

Whenever normal agencies prove inadequate to the task and it becomes necessary for the Executive Branch of the Federal Government to use its powers and authority to uphold Federal Courts, the President's responsibility is inescapable.

In accordance with that responsibility, I have today issued an Executive Order directing the use of troops under Federal authority to aid in the execution of Federal law at Little Rock, Arkansas. This became necessary when my Proclamation of yesterday was not observed, and the obstruction of justice still continues.

It is important that the reasons for my action be understood by all our citizens.

As you know, the Supreme Court of the United States has decided that separate public educational facilities for the races are inherently unequal and therefore compulsory school segregation laws are unconstitutional.

Our personal opinions about the decision have no bearing on the matter of enforcement; the responsibility and authority of the Supreme Court to interpret the Constitution are very clear. Local Federal Courts were instructed by the Supreme Court to issue such orders and decrees as might be necessary to achieve admission to public schools without regard to race—and with all deliberate speed.

During the past several years, many communities in our Southern States have instituted public school plans for gradual progress in the enrollment and attendance of school children of all races in order to bring themselves into compliance with the law of the land.

They thus demonstrated to the world that we are a nation in which laws, not men, are supreme.

I regret to say that this truth—the cornerstone of our liberties—was not observed in this instance.

It was my hope that this localized situation would be brought under control by city and State authorities. If the use of local police powers had been sufficient, our traditional method of leaving the problems in those hands would have been pursued. But when large gatherings of obstructionists made it impossible for the decrees of the Court to be carried out, both the law and the national interest demanded that the President take action.

Here is the sequence of events in the development of the Little Rock school case.

In May of 1955, the Little Rock School Board approved a moderate plan for the gradual desegregation of the public schools in that city. It provided that a start toward integration would be made at the present term in the high school, and that the plan would be in full operation by 1963. Here I might say that in a number of communities in Arkansas integration in the schools has already started and without violence of any kind. Now this Little Rock plan was challenged in the courts by some who believed that the period of time as proposed in the plan was too long.

The United States Court at Little Rock, which has supervisory responsibility under the law for the plan of desegregation in the public schools, dismissed the challenge, thus approving a gradual rather than an abrupt change from the existing system. The court found that the school board had acted in good faith in planning for a public school system free from racial discrimination.

Since that time, the court has on three separate occasions issued orders directing that the plan be carried out. All persons were instructed to refrain from interfering with the efforts of the school board to comply with the law.

Proper and sensible observance of the law then demanded the respectful obedience which the nation has a right to expect from all its people. This, unfortunately, has not been the case at Little Rock. Certain misguided persons, many of them imported into Little Rock by agitators, have insisted upon defying the law and have sought to bring it into disrepute. The orders of the court have thus been frustrated.

The very basis of our individual rights and freedoms rests upon the certainty that the President and the Executive Branch of Government will support and insure the carrying out of the decisions of the Federal Courts, even, when necessary with all the means at the President's command.

Unless the President did so, anarchy would result.

There would be no security for any except that which each one of us could provide for himself.

The interest of the nation in the proper fulfillment of the law's requirements cannot yield to opposition and demonstrations by some few persons.

Mob rule cannot be allowed to override the decisions of our courts.

Now, let me make it very clear that Federal troops are not being used to relieve local and state authorities of their primary duty to preserve the peace and order of the community. Nor are the troops there for the purpose of taking over the responsibility of the School Board and the other responsible local officials in running Central High School. The running of our school system and the maintenance of peace and order in each of our States are strictly local affairs and the Federal Government does not interfere except in a very few special cases and when requested by one of the several States. In the present case the troops are there, pursuant to law, solely for the purpose of preventing interference with the orders of the Court.

The proper use of the powers of the Executive Branch to enforce the orders of a Federal Court is limited to extraordinary and compelling circumstances. Manifestly, such an extreme situation has been created in Little Rock. This challenge must be met and with such measures as will preserve to the people as a whole their lawfully-protected rights in a climate permitting their free and fair exercise.

The overwhelming majority of our people in every section of the country are united in their respect for observance of the law—even in those cases where they may disagree with that law.

They deplore the call of extremists to violence.

The decision of the Supreme Court concerning school integration, of course, affects the South more seriously than it does other sections of the country. In that region I have many warm friends, some of them in the city of Little Rock. I have deemed it a great personal privilege to spend in our Southland tours of duty while in the military service and enjoyable recreational periods since that time.

So from intimate personal knowledge, I know that the overwhelming majority of the people in the South—including those of Arkansas and of Little Rock—are of good will, united in their efforts to preserve and respect the law even when they disagree with it.

They do not sympathize with mob rule. They, like the rest of our nation, have proved in two great wars their readiness to sacrifice for America.

A foundation of our American way of life is our national respect for law.

In the South, as elsewhere, citizens are keenly aware of the tremendous disservice that has been done to the people of Arkansas in the eyes of the nation, and that has been done to the nation in the eyes of the world.

At a time when we face grave situations abroad because of the hatred that Communism bears toward a system of government based on human rights, it would be difficult to exaggerate the harm that is being done to the prestige and influence, and indeed to the safety, of our nation and the world.

Our enemies are gloating over this incident and using it everywhere to misrepresent our whole nation. We are portrayed as a violator of those standards of conduct which the peoples of the world united to proclaim in the Charter of the United Nations. There they affirmed "faith in fundamental human rights" and "in the dignity and worth of the human person" and they did so "without distinction as to race, sex, language or religion."

And so, with deep confidence, I call upon the citizens of the State of Arkansas to assist in bringing to an immediate end all interference with the law and its processes. If resistance to the Federal Court orders ceases at once, the further presence of Federal troops will be unnecessary and the City of Little Rock will return to its normal habits of peace and order and a blot upon the fair name and high honor of our nation in the world will be removed.

Thus will be restored the image of America and of all its parts as one nation, indivisible, with liberty and justice for all.

Good night, and thank you very much.

DISCUSSION QUESTIONS

1. Why did President Eisenhower decide to send federal troops into Little Rock?
2. From this speech, can you determine Eisenhower's views on race? If so, what are they? If not, do they matter?

4

EXCERPTS FROM HEARINGS BEFORE THE UNITED STATES COMMISSION ON CIVIL RIGHTS, MONTGOMERY, ALABAMA (DECEMBER 8 AND 9, 1958)

TESTIMONY OF HOSEA GUICE, MILSTEAD, MACON COUNTY, ALA.

Vice Chairman [Robert G.] STOREY: Your name and age and place of residence, please.

Mr. GUICE: My name is Hosea Guice, 55 years old, born in Lee County, Ala.

Vice Chairman STOREY: On what date?

Mr. GUICE: On the 16th day of November 1904.

Vice Chairman STOREY: And how long have you lived in Alabama?

Mr. GUICE: In Alabama all of my life.

Vice Chairman STOREY: Where are you living now?

Mr. GUICE: In Macon County, Ala.

Vice Chairman STOREY: At what place?

Mr. GUICE: In Milstead Community, about 13 miles out from Tuskegee.

Vice Chairman STOREY: And how long have you lived there?

Mr. GUICE: Since 1942 at this particular place.

Vice Chairman STOREY: What is your business?

Mr. GUICE: Farming is my business.

Vice Chairman STOREY: How long have you been a farmer?

70

Mr. GUICE: All my life. Nothing else, only just little, minor jobs; but principally farming.

Vice Chairman STOREY: Is your wife living?

Mr. GUICE: She is.

Vice Chairman STOREY: Have you any children?

Mr. GUICE: Yes, sir.

Vice Chairman STOREY: How many?

Mr. GUICE: I got three daughters, and, of course, another boy was raised there with me, related. I raised him.

Vice Chairman STOREY: He is a relative, then?

Mr. GUICE: That's right.

Vice Chairman STOREY: Do you own your own farm?

Mr. GUICE: Yes sir; I do.

Vice Chairman STOREY: What size is it?

Mr. GUICE: A hundred and seventeen acres.

Vice Chairman STOREY: Do you mind saying whether it is paid for or not?

Mr. GUICE: Not quite paid for.

Vice Chairman STOREY: Still a mortgage on it?

Mr. GUICE: Yes; a little bit. A little bit.

Vice Chairman STOREY: Do you have your own farming equipment?

Mr. GUICE: I do.

Vice Chairman STOREY: Paid your taxes?

Mr. GUICE: Sure.

Vice Chairman STOREY: Got any mental or physical disabilities, as far as you know?

Mr. GUICE: No, sir. I haven't found them yet.

Vice Chairman STOREY: Have you ever been convicted of a crime?

Mr. GUICE: No, sir; I haven't.

Vice Chairman STOREY: What is your education, if any?

Mr. GUICE: Well, I finished the sixth grade. That's as far as I got—the sixth grade.

Vice Chairman STOREY: The sixth grade?

Mr. GUICE: Yes, sir.

Vice Chairman STOREY: Did you go to work after that?

Mr. GUICE: Well, I did. I went to work, the first farm work, see.

Vice Chairman STOREY: Can you read and write?

Mr. GUICE: I can.

Vice Chairman STOREY: Do you take any newspapers or magazines and read them?

Mr. GUICE: I sure do, every day.

Vice Chairman STOREY: Try to keep up with current events?

Mr. GUICE: I do, every day.

Vice Chairman STOREY: Are you a registered voter?

Mr. GUICE: No, sir; I am not.

Vice Chairman STOREY: Have you ever made application?

Mr. GUICE: Yes, sir.

Vice Chairman STOREY: When?

Mr. GUICE: The first application I made—the best I can recollect it was about 1954, I think it was, the first one.

Vice Chairman STOREY: Did you go to the board of registrars?

Mr. GUICE: Yes, sir.

Vice Chairman STOREY: In your county?

Mr. GUICE: Yes, sir; I did.

Vice Chairman STOREY: Did you go through a similar procedure as these other witnesses?

Mr. GUICE: I did, only except reading a portion of the Constitution. I wasn't asked to do that, see, but other than that I went through it.

Vice Chairman STOREY: And how long did you wait to see if you heard from that one before you did anything else?

Mr. GUICE: Well, I never did go back to see about the first one. However, I come up to all the requirements that I was asked to come up to, but I never did hear anything from it. I didn't nurse that first one that I made. I didn't go back to nurse it.

Vice Chairman STOREY: You didn't go back to nurse it?

Mr. GUICE: Yes, sir, the first time.

Vice Chairman STOREY: All right. What did you do? Did you make another application?

Mr. GUICE: I did.

Vice Chairman STOREY: When?

Mr. GUICE: I made an application—the best I can recollect it was shortly—it was the last of January of 1957, I think it was.

Vice Chairman STOREY: Did you fill out new forms?

Mr. GUICE: I did. I filled out another application.

Vice Chairman STOREY: Did they ask you to read or write anything?

Mr. GUICE: Nothing but to fill that application out. They didn't actually——

Vice Chairman STOREY: The one like we introduced here?

Mr. GUICE: That's right.

Vice Chairman STOREY: Did you ever hear anything from that application?

Mr. GUICE: No, sir.

Of course, I went back. After I thought I had given ample time, I——

Vice Chairman STOREY: About when did you go back?

Mr. GUICE: About 2 weeks later.

Vice Chairman STOREY: Did you talk to any of the election officials?

Mr. GUICE: Yes, sir. I talked to the gentleman—

Vice Chairman STOREY: Who?

Mr. GUICE: One of the members of the board there.

Vice Chairman STOREY: Who?

Mr. GUICE: In the person of Mr. Bentley.

Vice Chairman STOREY: All right. What did he tell you, if anything?

Mr. GUICE: He told me—I asked him about my application; I didn't come out, and so forth. He told me—he says, "Guice, you missed one little question."

I asked him did I have a chance to correct it. He said I did. "When we meet again, you'll have a chance to correct it."

That's the answer he give me.

Vice Chairman STOREY: Did you go back again?

Mr. GUICE: No, sir; I didn't go back.

Vice Chairman STOREY: Did he tell you what the particular thing you missed was?

Mr. GUICE: No, sir; he did not tell me that, and I——

Vice Chairman STOREY: And you haven't been back since?

Mr. GUICE: I didn't go back because I would read or hear when they were going to get together, and when I'd get on my way up there or when I would go they wouldn't be together then, and, just through a misunderstanding, they just kept me confused, you see.

Vice Chairman STOREY: How many times did you go back?

Mr. GUICE: One more time, after meeting him and talking to him. I went back for the particular purpose of investigating some more, but he——

Vice Chairman STOREY: Did you go back the time the board said it would be in session?

Mr. GUICE: I did.

Vice Chairman STOREY: Or that you learned it would be in session?

Mr. GUICE: That's right. That I learned they would be.

Vice Chairman STOREY: Were they in session when you went back?

Mr. GUICE: No, sir. They weren't in session that day.

Vice Chairman STOREY: Would you tell us why you want to vote?

Mr. GUICE: Well, I feel like I'm entitled to it. I have come up to the other requirements to make myself a citizen, and I feel I would like to be a registered voter; they ought to give that to me. It's like I want to become a part of the government activity, and so forth.

Vice Chairman STOREY. You don't have any connection with Tuskegee Institute?

Mr. GUICE: No, sir.

Vice Chairman STOREY: In any way?

Mr. GUICE: No. sir.

Vice Chairman STOREY: Any other questions?

Commissioner [Theodore M.] HESBURGH: Just one.
    Mr. Guice, have you paid taxes all your life?

Mr. GUICE: All my life?
    No, sir. Since 1942.

Commissioner HESBURGH: Since 1942?

Mr. GUICE: Every year since 1942 I have been paying taxes.

Vice Chairman STOREY: Any others?

Commissioner [J. Ernest] WILKINS: What do you raise on your farm, Mr. Guice?

Mr. GUICE: Principally cotton.

Commissioner WILKINS: Cotton?

Mr. GUICE: Cotton is the principal one. Corn and peas; all the things practically that goes with farming.

Commissioner WILKINS: Do you have any opinion, Mr. Guice, as to the reasons why you have never heard anything further about your application?

Mr. GUICE: Well, I have never been arrested and always has been a law-abiding citizen; to the best of my opinion has no mental deficiency, and my mind couldn't fall on nothing but only, since I come up to these other requirements, that I was just a Negro. That's all.

Commissioner WILKINS: All right. Thank you.

Vice Chairman STOREY: You may be excused.

TESTIMONY OF EUGENE W. ADAMS, TUSKEGEE, MACON COUNTY, ALA.

Vice Chairman STOREY: Will you please state your name, date of birth, place of birth, and place of residence?

Dr. ADAMS: My name is Eugene W. Adams. I was born in Guthrie, Okla., January 12, 1920. I am 38 years old. I live in Macon County, Tuskegee, Ala.

Vice Chairman STOREY: Are you married?

Dr. ADAMS: Yes, sir.

Vice Chairman STOREY: Any family besides your wife?

Dr. ADAMS: No, sir. Just my wife.

Vice Chairman STOREY: And do you own your own home?

Dr. ADAMS: Yes, sir; own my own home.

Vice Chairman STOREY: What is your business or profession?

Dr. ADAMS: I am in the employ of Tuskegee Institute as a teacher.

Vice Chairman STOREY: In what capacity?

Dr. ADAMS: As a teacher, sir.

Vice Chairman STOREY: In what department?

Dr. ADAMS: In the school of veterinary medicine.

Vice Chairman STOREY: Are you a graduate of any high school, universities, or colleges? If so, with what degrees?

Dr. ADAMS: I graduated from Wichita High School, North, in Wichita, Kans. I received the D.V.M. degree from Kansas State College, Manhattan, Kans. I received the master of science degree from Cornell in Ithaca, N.Y.

Vice Chairman STOREY: So, you are a doctor of veterinary medicine?

Dr. ADAMS: Yes.

Vice Chairman STOREY: And that is your profession?

Dr. ADAMS: Yes, sir; that is my profession.

Vice Chairman STOREY: How long have you been practicing that profession?

Dr. ADAMS: I graduated in 1944, and I have been practicing ever since.

Vice Chairman STOREY: Have you practiced in other States?

Dr. ADAMS: Yes, sir. In the State of Missouri.

Vice Chairman STOREY: Have you voted in any other States?

Dr. ADAMS: Yes, sir.

Vice Chairman STOREY: In what States?

Dr. ADAMS: In the State of Missouri I voted.

Vice Chairman STOREY: How long have you lived in Alabama?

Dr. ADAMS: I came to Alabama in August 1951.

Vice Chairman STOREY: And have you been living here since that time?

Dr. ADAMS: Yes, sir.

Vice Chairman STOREY: Do you have any mental or physical disability?

Dr. ADAMS: Not to my knowledge, sir.

Vice Chairman STOREY: Have you ever been convicted of a crime?

Dr. ADAMS: No, sir.

Vice Chairman STOREY: Have you ever applied to register?

Dr. ADAMS: Yes, sir.

Vice Chairman STOREY: When?

Dr. ADAMS: In the summer of 1953.

Vice Chairman STOREY: Did you go through a similar procedure as has been outlined here by other witnesses?

Dr. ADAMS: Yes, sir.

Vice Chairman STOREY: Did you hear anything from that application?

Dr. ADAMS: Not to this day, sir.

Vice Chairman STOREY: Have you been back?

Dr. ADAMS: I went back in 1954 and 1955, but the lines were so long at the time I went down I did not stay. So, I only got in one time. That was in 1953.

Vice Chairman STOREY: Only the one time?

Dr. ADAMS: Yes, sir, that I was actually entered.

Vice Chairman STOREY: And you never filed an additional formal application?

Dr. ADAMS: No, sir.

Vice Chairman STOREY: And you have heard nothing from it until this day?

Dr. ADAMS: No, sir; not a word.

Vice Chairman STOREY: Would you tell us why you want to vote?

Dr. ADAMS: Sir, I'm a property owner; I pay taxes, and I feel that it is my right to vote.

Vice Chairman STOREY: Do you know of any reason why you have not heard from the application?

Dr. ADAMS: I don't know of any reason, but I believe it's because I'm a Negro.

Vice Chairman STOREY: Any other question?

Chairman [John A.] HANNAH: Dr. Adams, what subjects do you teach in the college there?

Dr. ADAMS: I teach pathology.

Chairman HANNAH: You are in the department of pathology?

Dr. ADAMS: That's right. I head the department of pathology.

Vice Chairman STORE: Any other questions?

Commissioner WILKINS: Dr. Adams, I believe you are able to read and interpret the provisions of the United States Constitution?

Dr. ADAMS: I think so, sir.

Commissioner WILKINS: Did you have any conversation at all with the registrars?

Dr. ADAMS: No, sir; none whatsoever. None whatsoever.

Commissioner WILKINS: And they never said anything about your application when you handed it in?

Dr. ADAMS: No, sir.

Commissioner WILKINS: And you have never heard from them?

Dr. ADAMS: Not a word.

Commissioner WILKINS: That is all.

Commissioner HESBURGH: Dr. Adams, do you know why the American Revolution was fought?

Dr. ADAMS: Why it was fought?

Commissioner HESBURGH: That is not a trick question.

Dr. ADAMS: Well, according to American history, it was fought to free this country from England.

Commissioner HESBURGH: Do you remember the famous saying?

Dr. ADAMS: "Taxation without representation"——

Vice Chairman STOREY: I don't know whether all can hear you or not.

Commissioner HESBURGH: Louder.

Dr. ADAMS: "Taxation without representation"——

Commissioner HESBURGH: "★ ★ ★ is tyranny."

Dr. ADAMS: "Is tyranny"; yes, sir.

Commissioner HESBURGH: You have been paying taxes?

Dr. ADAMS: I have been paying taxes ever since I am old enough to.

Vice Chairman STOREY: Any other question?
If not, you are excused.

DISCUSSION QUESTIONS

1. Why did the civil rights movement consider the right to vote so important?
2. Hosea Guice argues that he should vote because he pays taxes. If taxation is the basis of representation, should those who are too poor to pay income or property taxes be allowed to vote?

5

THE FBI AND MARTIN LUTHER KING, JR. (JANUARY 17 AND 18, 1963)

MEMORANDUM TO MR. [ALAN H.] BELMONT FROM [ALEX] ROSEN CONCERNING RACIAL SITUATION IN ALBANY, GEORGIA (JANUARY 17, 1963)

Reference is made to the memorandum of Mr. [Cartha D.] De-Loach to Mr. [John P.] Mohr, January 15, 1963, pointing out the attempts made to interview Reverend Martin Luther King, Jr., to give him the truth concerning the role of the FBI in the Albany situation. Numerous attempts were made to contact him and he has completely evaded all attempts to reach him to set the record straight.

King's comments have been previously brought to the attention of Mr. Berl I. Bernhard, Staff Director of the U.S. Commission on Civil Rights, and it was pointed out to him that there is no basis in fact for King's remarks. In addition, it was pointed out that four of the five Resident Agents at Albany are from northern states and one is from Georgia.

As has been indicated by Mr. DeLoach's memorandum, interviews with publishers of the newspapers who carried Reverend King's lies have been conducted and they have been set straight. As pointed out, no further need to contact Reverend Mr. King exists inasmuch as he obviously does not desire to be given the truth. The fact that he is a vicious liar is amply demonstrated in the fact he constantly associates with and takes instructions from Stanley Levison who is a hidden member of the Communist Party in New York.

RECOMMENDATION:

In view of the conduct of Reverend Mr. King in completely evading any attempts to learn the truth of this Bureau's role in the Albany situation, it is recommended that in addition to the action taken above, the attached letters to the Attorney General and to Mr. Bernhard be sent pointing out the evasive conduct of King.

MEMORANDUM TO THE ATTORNEY GENERAL [ROBERT F. KENNEDY] FROM THE DIRECTOR OF THE FBI [J. EDGAR HOOVER] CONCERNING THE RACIAL SITUATION IN ALBANY, GEORGIA (JANUARY 18, 1963)

Numerous attempts have been made by officials of this Bureau to contact Reverend Martin Luther King, Jr., to point out to him the inaccuracies in his unfounded allegations about the work of this Bureau in connection with Albany, Georgia, which allegations appeared in the November 19, 1962, issue of "The New York Times." It is obvious to the Bureau that Reverend Mr. King has evaded contact and has no desire to be told the true facts concerning this situation.

An attempt was made by an official of this Bureau to contact Reverend Mr. King on November 27, 1962. Upon learning the identity of the caller, his secretary advised that Reverend Mr. King was "off in another building writing a book." She further stated that he preferred not to be disturbed and it would be impossible to talk with him.

Another attempt was made on November 28, 1962, and it was ascertained that Reverend Mr. King had left instructions with his secretary that he would not have time for an interview and that he was moving-around the country. The secretary further advised that Reverend Mr. King would call this Bureau when he was willing to sit down for an interview. He has not called since that date.

DISCUSSION QUESTIONS

1. Do you believe that the FBI was justified in targeting Martin Luther King for surveillance? Explain your answer.
2. What role did presidents John Kennedy and Lyndon Johnson play in the FBI's decision to eavesdrop?

6

JOHN F. KENNEDY'S RADIO AND TELEVISION REPORT TO THE AMERICAN PEOPLE ON CIVIL RIGHTS (JUNE 11, 1963)

Good evening, my fellow citizens:

This afternoon, following a series of threats and defiant statements, the presence of Alabama National Guardsmen was required on the University of Alabama to carry out the final and unequivocal order of the United States District Court of the Northern District of Alabama. That order called for the admission of two clearly qualified young Alabama residents who happened to have been born Negro.

That they were admitted peacefully on the campus is due in good measure to the conduct of the students of the University of Alabama, who met their responsibilities in a constructive way.

I hope that every American, regardless of where he lives, will stop and examine his conscience about this and other related incidents. This Nation was founded by men of many nations and backgrounds. It was founded on the principle that all men are created equal, and that the rights of every man are diminished when the rights of one man are threatened.

Today we are committed to a worldwide struggle to promote and protect the rights of all who wish to be free. And when Americans are sent to Viet-Nam or West Berlin, we do not ask for whites only. It ought to be possible, therefore, for American students of any color to attend any public institution they select without having to be backed up by troops.

It ought to be possible for American consumers of any color to receive equal service in places of public accommodation, such as hotels and restaurants and theaters and retail stores, without being forced to resort to demonstrations in the street, and it ought to be possible for American citizens of any color to register and to vote in a free election without interference or fear of reprisal.

It ought to be possible, in short, for every American to enjoy the privileges of being American without regard to his race or his color. In short, every American ought to have the right to be treated as he would wish to be treated, as one would wish his children to be treated. But this is not the case.

The Negro baby born in America today, regardless of the section of the Nation in which he is born, has about one-half as much chance of completing a high school as a white baby born in the same place on the same day, one-third as much chance of completing college, one-third as much chance of becoming a professional man, twice as much chance of becoming unemployed, about one-seventh as much chance of earning $10,000 a year, a life expectancy which is 7 years shorter, and the prospects of earning only half as much.

This is not a sectional issue. Difficulties over segregation and discrimination exist in every city, in every State of the Union, producing in many cities a rising tide of discontent that threatens the public safety. Nor is this a partisan issue. In a time of domestic crisis men of good will and generosity should be able to unite regardless of party or politics. This is not even a legal or legislative issue alone. It is better to settle these matters in the courts than on the streets, and new laws are needed at every level, but law alone cannot make men see right.

We are confronted primarily with a moral issue. It is as old as the scriptures and is as clear as the American Constitution.

The heart of the question is whether all Americans are to be afforded equal rights and equal opportunities, whether we are going to treat our fellow Americans as we want to be treated. If an American, because his skin is dark, cannot eat lunch in a restaurant open to the public, if he cannot send his children to the best public school available, if he cannot vote for the public officials who represent him, if, in short, he cannot enjoy the full and free life which all of us want, then who among us would be content to have the color of his skin changed and stand in his place? Who among us would then be content with the counsels of patience and delay?

One hundred years of delay have passed since President Lincoln freed the slaves, yet their heirs, their grandsons, are not fully free. They are not yet freed from the bonds of injustice. They are not yet freed from social and economic oppression. And this Nation, for all its hopes and all its boasts, will not be fully free until all its citizens are free.

We preach freedom around the world, and we mean it, and we cherish our freedom here at home, but are we to say to the world, and much more importantly, to each other that this is a land of the free except for the Negroes; that we have no second-class citizens except Negroes; that we have no class or caste system, no ghettoes, no master race except with respect to Negroes?

Now the time has come for this Nation to fulfill its promise. The events in Birmingham and elsewhere have so increased the cries for equality that no city or State or legislative body can prudently choose to ignore them.

The fires of frustration and discord are burning in every city, North and South, where legal remedies are not at hand. Redress is sought in the streets, in demonstrations, parades, and protests which create tensions and threaten violence and threaten lives.

We face, therefore, a moral crisis as a country and as a people. It cannot be met by repressive police action. It cannot be left to increased demonstrations in the streets. It cannot be quieted by token moves or talk. It is a time to act in the Congress, in your State and local legislative body and, above all, in all of our daily lives.

It is not enough to pin the blame on others, to say this is a problem of one section of the country or another, or deplore the fact that we face. A great change is at hand, and our task, our obligation, is to make that revolution, that change, peaceful and constructive for all.

Those who do nothing are inviting shame as well as violence. Those who act boldly are recognizing right as well as reality.

Next week I shall ask the Congress of the United States to act, to make a commitment it has not fully made in this century to the proposition that race has no place in American life or law. The Federal judiciary has upheld that proposition in a series of forthright cases. The executive branch has adopted that proposition in the conduct of its affairs, including the employment of Federal personnel, the use of Federal facilities, and the sale of federally financed housing.

But there are other necessary measures which only the Congress can provide, and they must be provided at this session. The old code of equity law under which we live commands for every wrong a remedy, but in too many communities, in too many parts of the country, wrongs are inflicted on Negro citizens and there are no remedies at law. Unless the Congress acts, their only remedy is in the street.

I am, therefore, asking the Congress to enact legislation giving all Americans the right to be served in facilities which are open to the public—hotels, restaurants, theaters, retail stores, and similar establishments.

This seems to me to be an elementary right. Its denial is an arbitrary indignity that no American in 1963 should have to endure, but many do.

I have recently met with scores of business leaders urging them to take voluntary action to end this discrimination and I have been encouraged by their response, and in the last 2 weeks over 75 cities have seen progress made in desegregating these kinds of facilities. But many are unwilling to act alone, and for this reason, nationwide legislation is needed if we are to move this problem from the streets to the courts.

I am also asking Congress to authorize the Federal Government to participate more fully in lawsuits designed to end segregation in public education. We have succeeded in persuading many districts to desegregate voluntarily. Dozens have admitted Negroes without violence. Today a Negro is attending a State-supported institution in every one of our 50 States, but the pace is very slow.

Too many Negro children entering segregated grade schools at the time of the Supreme Court's decision 9 years ago will enter segregated high schools this fall, having suffered a loss which can never be restored. The lack of an adequate education denies the Negro a chance to get a decent job.

The orderly implementation of the Supreme Court decision, therefore, cannot be left solely to those who may not have the economic resources to carry the legal action or who may be subject to harassment.

Other features will be also requested, including greater protection for the right to vote. But legislation, I repeat, cannot solve this problem alone. It must be solved in the homes of every American in every community across our country.

In this respect, I want to pay tribute to those citizens North and South who have been working in their communities to make life better for all. They are acting not out of a sense of legal duty but out of a sense of human decency.

Like our soldiers and sailors in all parts of the world they are meeting freedom's challenge on the firing line, and I salute them for their honor and their courage.

My fellow Americans, this is a problem which faces us all—in every city of the North as well as the South. Today there are Negroes unemployed, two or three times as many compared to whites, inadequate in education, moving into the large cities, unable to find work, young people particularly out of work without hope, denied equal rights, denied the opportunity to eat at a restaurant or lunch counter or go to a movie theater, denied the right to a decent education, denied almost today the right to attend a State university even though qualified. It seems to me that these are matters which concern us all, not merely Presidents or Congressmen or Governors, but every citizen of the United States.

This is one country. It has become one country because all of us and all the people who came here had an equal chance to develop their talents.

We cannot say to 10 percent of the population that you can't have that right; that your children can't have the chance to develop whatever talents they have; that the only way that they are going to get their rights is to go into the streets and demonstrate. I think we owe them and we owe ourselves a better country than that.

Therefore, I am asking for your help in making it easier for us to move ahead and to provide the kind of equality of treatment which we would want ourselves; to give a chance for every child to be educated to the limit of his talents.

As I have said before, not every child has an equal talent or an equal ability or an equal motivation, but they should have the equal right to develop their talent and their ability and their motivation, to make something of themselves.

We have a right to expect that the Negro community will be responsible, will uphold the law, but they have a right to expect that the law will be fair, that the Constitution will be color blind, as Justice Harlan said at the turn of the century.

This is what we are talking about and this is a matter which concerns this country and what it stands for, and in meeting it I ask the support of all our citizens.

Thank you very much.

DISCUSSION QUESTIONS

1. Why did President Kennedy send in federal forces to the University of Alabama? How does his reasoning compare with Eisenhower's in Little Rock?
2. Can you tell from this speech Kennedy's views on race? If so, how can you tell?

7

LETTER FROM WILEY A. BRANTON, DIRECTOR, VOTER EDUCATION PROJECT, TO AARON HENRY AND ROBERT MOSES (NOVEMBER 12, 1963)

Gentlemen:

This will confirm my separate conversations with each of you last week in New York in which I informed you that VEP has reluctantly come to the decision that we cannot give any further financial support to voter registration programs in Mississippi for the balance of this fiscal year which ends March 31, 1964. We feel obligated to give some minimum support to the continued operation of your COFO office in Greenwood and we have decided to contribute the sum of $250 per month for a period of four months beginning December 1, 1963. This will be for the sole purpose of helping you to maintain your Greenwood office.

We deeply regret the fact that we are being forced to suspend our financial contributions in Mississippi and we want to assure you that this decision in no way reflects unfavorably on the cooperation all of you have shown to VEP nor does it indicate any lack of interest or appreciation for what you are doing.

Our decision to suspend financial support at this time is dictated primarily by reason of the fact that we try to maintain some equitable allocation of funds on a geographic basis in proportion to the total number of unregistered voters and we find that we have spent far more money in

Mississippi than we have in any other state and the Mississippi expenditures exceed by far the amount available under our VEP formula. To continue to support projects in Mississippi would necessitate a reduction of effort in other areas where meaningful registration results can now be achieved.

Of almost equal importance to our decision is the fact that the Justice Department has failed to get any meaningful decrees from any of the voter suits which have been filed in Mississippi and we know that until and unless favorable decrees are rendered and then vigorously imposed we will not be able to get many people registered successfully. We are also very concerned about the failure of the federal government to protect the people who have sought to register and vote or who are working actively in getting others to register and we certainly commend the thousands of people who have constantly braved the insults and harassment, intimidation and violence in their efforts to become first class citizens.

VEP is now scheduled to end sometime next year and I do not know if we will be in a position to make any further contributions before we wind up our field programs but if we are able to get new funds for our third and final fiscal year then we will probably be able to resume some financial support in Mississippi next spring.

Very truly yours,
Wiley A. Branton

DISCUSSION QUESTIONS

1. Why did Wiley Branton blame the Justice Department for his decision to suspend Voter Education Project funds in Mississippi?
2. Why didn't the federal government provide protection for voting rights workers whereas it did so for those seeking to integrate Central High School in Little Rock and the University of Alabama?

8

LYNDON B. JOHNSON'S SPECIAL MESSAGE TO THE CONGRESS: THE AMERICAN PROMISE (MARCH 15, 1965)

Mr. Speaker, Mr. President, Members of the Congress:

I speak tonight for the dignity of man and the destiny of democracy.

I urge every member of both parties, Americans of all religions and of all colors, from every section of this country, to join me in that cause.

At times history and fate meet at a single time in a single place to shape a turning point in man's unending search for freedom. So it was at Lexington and Concord. So it was a century ago at Appomattox. So it was last week in Selma, Alabama.

There, long-suffering men and women peacefully protested the denial of their rights as Americans. Many were brutally assaulted. One good man, a man of God, was killed.

There is no cause for pride in what has happened in Selma. There is no cause for self-satisfaction in the long denial of equal rights of millions of Americans. But there is cause for hope and for faith in our democracy in what is happening here tonight.

For the cries of pain and the hymns and protests of oppressed people have summoned into convocation all the majesty of this great Government—the Government of the greatest Nation on earth.

Our mission is at once the oldest and the most basic of this country: to right wrong, to do justice, to serve man.

In our time we have come to live with moments of great crisis. Our lives have been marked with debate about great issues; issues of war and peace, issues of prosperity and depression. But rarely in any time does an issue lay bare the secret heart of America itself. Rarely are we met with a challenge, not to our growth or abundance, our welfare or our security, but rather to the values and the purposes and the meaning of our beloved Nation.

The issue of equal rights for American Negroes is such an issue. And should we defeat every enemy, should we double our wealth and conquer the stars, and still be unequal to this issue, then we will have failed as a people and as a nation.

For with a country as with a person, "What is a man profited, if he shall gain the whole world, and lose his own soul?"

There is no Negro problem. There is no Southern problem. There is no Northern problem. There is only an American problem. And we are met here tonight as Americans—not as Democrats or Republicans—we are met here as Americans to solve that problem.

This was the first nation in the history of the world to be founded with a purpose. The great phrases of that purpose still sound in every American heart, North and South: "All men are created equal"— "government by consent of the governed"—"give me liberty or give me death." Well, those are not just clever words, or those are not just empty theories. In their name Americans have fought and died for two centuries, and tonight around the world they stand there as guardians of our liberty, risking their lives.

Those words are a promise to every citizen that he shall share in the dignity of man. This dignity cannot be found in a man's possessions; it cannot be found in his power, or in his position. It really rests on his right to be treated as a man equal in opportunity to all others. It says that he shall share in freedom, he shall choose his leaders, educate his children, and provide for his family according to his ability and his merits as a human being.

To apply any other test—to deny a man his hopes because of his color or race, his religion or the place of his birth—is not only to do injustice, it is to deny America and to dishonor the dead who gave their lives for American freedom.

THE RIGHT TO VOTE

Our fathers believed that if this noble view of the rights of man was to flourish, it must be rooted in democracy. The most basic right of all was the right to choose your own leaders. The history of this country, in large measure, is the history of the expansion of that right to all of our people.

Many of the issues of civil rights are very complex and most difficult. But about this there can and should be no argument. Every American citizen must have an equal right to vote. There is no reason which can excuse the denial of that right. There is no duty which weighs more heavily on us than the duty we have to ensure that right.

Yet the harsh fact is that in many places in this country men and women are kept from voting simply because they are Negroes.

Every device of which human ingenuity is capable has been used to deny this right. The Negro citizen may go to register only to be told that the day is wrong, or the hour is late, or the official in charge is absent. And if he persists, and if he manages to present himself to the registrar, he may be disqualified because he did not spell out his middle name or because he abbreviated a word on the application.

And if he manages to fill out an application he is given a test. The registrar is the sole judge of whether he passes this test. He may be asked to recite the entire Constitution, or explain the most complex provisions of State law. And even a college degree cannot be used to prove that he can read and write.

For the fact is that the only way to pass these barriers is to show a white skin.

Experience has clearly shown that the existing process of law cannot overcome systematic and ingenious discrimination. No law that we now have on the books—and I have helped to put three of them there—can ensure the right to vote when local officials are determined to deny it.

In such a case our duty must be clear to all of us. The Constitution says that no person shall be kept from voting because of his race or his color. We have all sworn an oath before God to support and to defend that Constitution. We must now act in obedience to that oath.

GUARANTEEING THE RIGHT TO VOTE

Wednesday I will send to Congress a law designed to eliminate illegal barriers to the right to vote.

The broad principles of that bill will be in the hands of the Democratic and Republican leaders tomorrow. After they have reviewed it, it will come here formally as a bill. I am grateful for this opportunity to come here tonight at the invitation of the leadership to reason with my friends, to give them my views, and to visit with my former colleagues.

I have had prepared a more comprehensive analysis of the legislation which I had intended to transmit to the clerk tomorrow but which I will submit to the clerks tonight. But I want to really discuss with you now briefly the main proposals of this legislation.

This bill will strike down restrictions to voting in all elections—Federal, State, and local—which have been used to deny Negroes the right to vote.

This bill will establish a simple, uniform standard which cannot be used, however ingenious the effort, to flout our Constitution.

It will provide for citizens to be registered by officials of the United States Government if the State officials refuse to register them.

It will eliminate tedious, unnecessary lawsuits which delay the right to vote.

Finally, this legislation will ensure that properly registered individuals are not prohibited from voting.

I will welcome the suggestions from all of the Members of Congress—I have no doubt that I will get some—on ways and means to strengthen this law and to make it effective. But experience has plainly shown that this is the only path to carry out the command of the Constitution.

To those who seek to avoid action by their National Government in their own communities; who want to and who seek to maintain purely local control over elections, the answer is simple:

Open your polling places to all your people.

Allow men and women to register and vote whatever the color of their skin.

Extend the rights of citizenship to every citizen of this land.

THE NEED FOR ACTION

There is no constitutional issue here. The command of the Constitution is plain.

There is no moral issue. It is wrong—deadly wrong—to deny any of your fellow Americans the right to vote in this country.

There is no issue of States rights or national rights. There is only the struggle for human rights.

I have not the slightest doubt what will be your answer.

The last time a President sent a civil rights bill to the Congress it contained a provision to protect voting rights in Federal elections. That civil rights bill was passed after 8 long months of debate. And when that bill came to my desk from the Congress for my signature, the heart of the voting provision had been eliminated.

This time, on this issue, there must be no delay, no hesitation and no compromise with our purpose.

We cannot, we must not, refuse to protect the right of every American to vote in every election that he may desire to participate in. And we ought not and we cannot and we must not wait another 8 months before we get a bill. We have already waited a hundred years and more, and the time for waiting is gone.

So I ask you to join me in working long hours—nights and weekends, if necessary—to pass this bill. And I don't make that request lightly. For from the window where I sit with the problems of our country I recognize that outside this chamber is the outraged conscience of a nation, the grave concern of many nations, and the harsh judgment of history on our acts.

WE SHALL OVERCOME

But even if we pass this bill, the battle will not be over. What happened in Selma is part of a far larger movement which reaches into every section and State of America. It is the effort of American Negroes to secure for themselves the full blessings of American life.

Their cause must be our cause too. Because it is not just Negroes, but really it is all of us, who must overcome the crippling legacy of bigotry and injustice.

And we shall overcome.

As a man whose roots go deeply into Southern soil I know how agonizing racial feelings are. I know how difficult it is to reshape the attitudes and the structure of our society.

But a century has passed, more than a hundred years, since the Negro was freed. And he is not fully free tonight.

It was more than a hundred years ago that Abraham Lincoln, a great President of another party, signed the Emancipation Proclamation, but emancipation is a proclamation and not a fact.

A century has passed, more than a hundred years, since equality was promised. And yet the Negro is not equal.

A century has passed since the day of promise. And the promise is unkept.

The time of justice has now come. I tell you that I believe sincerely that no force can hold it back. It is right in the eyes of man and God that it should come. And when it does, I think that day will brighten the lives of every American.

For Negroes are not the only victims. How many white children have gone uneducated, how many white families have lived in stark poverty, how many white lives have been scarred by fear, because we have wasted our energy and our substance to maintain the barriers of hatred and terror?

So I say to all of you here, and to all in the Nation tonight, that those who appeal to you to hold on to the past do so at the cost of denying you your future.

This great, rich, restless country can offer opportunity and education and hope to all: black and white, North and South, sharecropper and city dweller. These are the enemies: poverty, ignorance, disease. They are the enemies and not our fellow man, not our neighbor. And these enemies too, poverty, disease and ignorance, we shall overcome.

AN AMERICAN PROBLEM

Now let none of us in any sections look with prideful righteousness on the troubles in another section, or on the problems of our neighbors. There is really no part of America where the promise of equality has been fully kept. In Buffalo as well as in Birmingham, in Philadelphia as well as in Selma, Americans are struggling for the fruits of freedom.

This is one Nation. What happens in Selma or in Cincinnati is a matter of legitimate concern to every American. But let each of us look within our own hearts and our own communities, and let each of us put our shoulder to the wheel to root out injustice wherever it exists.

As we meet here in this peaceful, historic chamber tonight, men from the South, some of whom were at Iwo Jima, men from the North who have carried Old Glory to far corners of the world and brought it back without a stain on it, men from the East and from the West, are all fighting together without regard to religion, or color, or region, in Viet-Nam. Men from every region fought for us across the world 20 years ago.

And in these common dangers and these common sacrifices the South made its contribution of honor and gallantry no less than any other region of the great Republic—and in some instances, a great many of them, more.

And I have not the slightest doubt that good men from everywhere in this country, from the Great Lakes to the Gulf of Mexico, from the Golden Gate to the harbors along the Atlantic, will rally together now in this cause to vindicate the freedom of all Americans. For all of us owe this duty; and I believe that all of us will respond to it.

Your President makes that request of every American.

PROGRESS THROUGH THE DEMOCRATIC PROCESS

The real hero of this struggle is the American Negro. His actions and protests, his courage to risk safety and even to risk his life, have awakened the conscience of this Nation. His demonstrations have been designed to call attention to injustice, designed to provoke change, designed to stir reform.

He has called upon us to make good the promise of America. And who among us can say that we would have made the same progress were it not for his persistent bravery, and his faith in American democracy.

For at the real heart of battle for equality is a deep-seated belief in the democratic process. Equality depends not on the force of arms or tear gas but upon the force of moral right; not on recourse to violence but on respect for law and order.

There have been many pressures upon your President and there will be others as the days come and go. But I pledge you tonight that we intend to fight this battle where it should be fought: in the courts, and in the Congress, and in the hearts of men.

We must preserve the right of free speech and the right of free assembly. But the right of free speech does not carry with it, as has been said, the right to holler fire in a crowded theater. We must preserve the right to free assembly, but free assembly does not carry with it the right to block public thoroughfares to traffic.

We do have a right to protest, and a right to march under conditions that do not infringe the constitutional rights of our neighbors. And I intend to protect all those rights as long as I am permitted to serve in this office.

We will guard against violence, knowing it strikes from our hands the very weapons which we seek—progress, obedience to law, and belief in American values.

In Selma as elsewhere we seek and pray for peace. We seek order. We seek unity. But we will not accept the pace of stifled rights, or the order imposed by fear, or the unity that stifles protest. For peace cannot be purchased at the cost of liberty.

In Selma tonight, as in every—and we had a good day there—as in every city, we are working for just and peaceful settlement. We must all remember that after this speech I am making tonight, after the police and the FBI and the Marshals have all gone, and after you have promptly passed this bill, the people of Selma and the other cities of the Nation must still live and work together. And when the attention of the Nation has gone elsewhere they must try to heal the wounds and to build a new community.

This cannot be easily done on a battleground of violence, as the history of the South itself shows. It is in recognition of this that men of both races have shown such an outstandingly impressive responsibility in recent days—last Tuesday, again today.

RIGHTS MUST BE OPPORTUNITIES

The bill that I am presenting to you will be known as a civil rights bill. But, in a larger sense, most of the program I am recommending is a civil rights program. Its object is to open the city of hope to all people of all races.

Because all Americans just must have the right to vote. And we are going to give them that right.

All Americans must have the privileges of citizenship regardless of race. And they are going to have those privileges of citizenship regardless of race.

But I would like to caution you and remind you that to exercise these privileges takes much more than just legal right. It requires a trained mind and a healthy body. It requires a decent home, and the chance to find a job, and the opportunity to escape from the clutches of poverty.

Of course, people cannot contribute to the Nation if they are never taught to read or write, if their bodies are stunted from hunger, if their sickness goes untended, if their life is spent in hopeless poverty just drawing a welfare check.

So we want to open the gates to opportunity. But we are also going to give all our people, black and white, the help that they need to walk through those gates.

THE PURPOSE OF THIS GOVERNMENT

My first job after college was as a teacher in Cotulla, Tex., in a small Mexican-American school. Few of them could speak English, and I couldn't speak much Spanish. My students were poor and they often came to class without breakfast, hungry. They knew even in their youth the pain of prejudice. They never seemed to know why people disliked them. But they knew it was so, because I saw it in their eyes. I often walked home late in the afternoon, after the classes were finished, wishing there was more that I could do. But all I knew was to teach them the little that I knew, hoping that it might help them against the hardships that lay ahead.

Somehow you never forget what poverty and hatred can do when you see its scars on the hopeful face of a young child.

I never thought then, in 1928, that I would be standing here in 1965. It never even occurred to me in my fondest dreams that I might have the chance to help the sons and daughters of those students and to help people like them all over this country.

But now I do have that chance—and I'll let you in on a secret—I mean to use it. And I hope that you will use it with me.

This is the richest and most powerful country which ever occupied the globe. The might of past empires is little compared to ours. But I do not want to be the President who built empires, or sought grandeur, or extended dominion.

I want to be the President who educated young children to the wonders of their world. I want to be the President who helped to feed the hungry and to prepare them to be taxpayers instead of taxeaters.

I want to be the President who helped the poor to find their own way and who protected the right of every citizen to vote in every election.

I want to be the President who helped to end hatred among his fellow men and who promoted love among the people of all races and all regions and all parties.

I want to be the President who helped to end war among the brothers of this earth.

And so at the request of your beloved Speaker and the Senator from Montana; the majority leader, the Senator from Illinois; the minority leader, Mr. McCulloch, and other Members of both parties, I came here tonight—not as President Roosevelt came down one time in person to veto a bonus bill, not as President Truman came down one time to urge the passage of a railroad bill—but I came down here to ask you to share this task with me and to share it with the people that we both work for. I want this to be the Congress, Republicans and Democrats alike, which did all these things for all these people.

Beyond this great chamber, out yonder in 50 States, are the people that we serve. Who can tell what deep and unspoken hopes are in their hearts tonight as they sit there and listen. We all can guess, from our own lives, how difficult they often find their own pursuit of happiness, how many problems each little family has. They look most of all to themselves for their futures. But I think that they also look to each of us.

Above the pyramid on the great seal of the United States it says—in Latin—"God has favored our undertaking."

God will not favor everything that we do. It is rather our duty to divine His will. But I cannot help believing that He truly understands and that He really favors the undertaking that we begin here tonight.

DISCUSSION QUESTIONS

1. Why did President Johnson believe the right to vote is the most important civil right?
2. What is the significance of Johnson using the phrase, "We shall overcome"?

9

EXCERPT FROM THE INTRODUCTION TO THE *REPORT OF THE NATIONAL ADVISORY COMMISSION ON CIVIL DISORDERS* (MARCH 1968)

The summer of 1967 again brought racial disorders to American cities, and with them shock, fear and bewilderment to the nation.

The worst came during a two-week period in July, first in Newark and then in Detroit. Each set off a chain reaction in neighboring communities.

On July 28, 1967, the President of the United States established this Commission and directed us to answer three basic questions:

What happened?
Why did it happen?
What can be done to prevent it from happening again?

To respond to these questions, we have undertaken a broad range of studies and investigations. We have visited the riot cities; we have heard many witnesses; we have sought the counsel of experts across the country.

This is our basic conclusion: Our nation is moving toward two societies, one black, one white—separate and unequal.

Reaction to last summer's disorders has quickened the movement and deepened the division. Discrimination and segregation have long permeated much of American life; they now threaten the future of every American.

This deepening racial division is not inevitable. The movement apart can be reversed. Choice is still possible. Our principal task is to define that choice and to press for a national resolution.

To pursue our present course will involve the continuing polarization of the American community and, ultimately, the destruction of basic democratic values.

The alternative is not blind repression or capitulation to lawlessness. It is the realization of common opportunities for all within a single society.

This alternative will require a commitment to national action—compassionate, massive and sustained, backed by the resources of the most powerful and the richest nation on this earth. From every American it will require new attitudes, new understanding, and, above all, new will.

The vital needs of the nation must be met; hard choices must be made, and if necessary, new taxes enacted.

Violence cannot build a better society. Disruption and disorder nourish repression, not justice. They strike at the freedom of every citizen. The community cannot—it will not—tolerate coercion and mob rule.

Violence and destruction must be ended—in the streets of the ghetto and in the lives of people.

Segregation and poverty have created in the racial ghetto a destructive environment totally unknown to most white Americans.

What white Americans have never fully understood—but what the Negro can never forget—is that white society is deeply implicated in the ghetto. White institutions created it, white institutions maintain it, and white society condones it.

It is time now to turn with all the purpose at our command to the major unfinished business of this nation. It is time to adopt strategies for action that will produce quick and visible progress. It is time to make good the promises of American democracy to all citizens—urban and rural, white and black, Spanish-surname, American Indian, and every minority group.

Our recommendations embrace three basic principles:

- To mount programs on a scale equal to the dimension of the problems;

- To aim these programs for high impact in the immediate future in order to close the gap between promise and performance;
- To undertake new initiatives and experiments that can change the system of failure and frustration that now dominates the ghetto and weakens our society.

These programs will require unprecedented levels of funding and performance, but they neither probe deeper nor demand more than the problems which called them forth. There can be no higher priority for national action and no higher claim on the nation's conscience.

We issue this Report now, four months before the date called for by the President. Much remains that can be learned. Continued study is essential.

As Commissioners we have worked together with a sense of the greatest urgency and have sought to compose whatever differences exist among us. Some differences remain. But the gravity of the problem and the pressing need for action are too clear to allow further delay in the issuance of this Report.

DISCUSSION QUESTIONS

1. How effective were the urban uprisings as a political tactic?
2. What difference does it make to use the term "riots" instead of "civil disorders" and "rebellions"?

10

MARTIN LUTHER KING, JR.'S LAST SCLC PRESIDENTIAL ADDRESS: WHERE DO WE GO FROM HERE? (1967)

Now, in order to answer the question, "Where do we go from here?" which is our theme, we must first honestly recognize where we are now. When the Constitution was written, a strange formula to determine taxes and representation declared that the Negro was sixty percent of a person. Today another curious formula seems to declare that he is fifty percent of a person. Of the good things in life, the Negro has approximately one half those of whites. Of the bad things of life, he has twice those of whites. Thus half of all Negroes live in substandard housing. And Negroes have half the income of whites. When we view the negative experiences of life, the Negro has a double share. There are twice as many unemployed. The rate of infant mortality among Negroes is double that of whites and there are twice as many Negroes dying in Vietnam as whites in proportion to their size in the population.

In other spheres, the figures are equally alarming. In elementary schools, Negroes lag one to three years behind whites, and their segregated schools receive substantially less money per student than the white schools. One-twentieth as many Negroes as whites attend college. Of employed Negroes, seventy-five percent hold menial jobs.

This is where we are. Where do we go from here? First, we must massively assert our dignity and worth. We must stand up amidst a system that still oppresses us and develop an unassailable and majestic sense of values. We must no longer be ashamed of being black. The job of arousing manhood within a people that have been taught for so many centuries that they are nobody is not easy.

Even semantics have conspired to make that which is black seem ugly and degrading. In Roget's *Thesaurus* there are 120 synonyms for blackness and at least sixty of them are offensive, as for example, blot, soot, grim, devil and foul. And there are some 134 synonyms for whiteness and all are favorable, expressed in such words as purity, cleanliness, chastity and innocence. A white lie is better than a black lie. The most degenerate member of a family is a "black sheep." Ossie Davis has suggested that maybe the English language should be reconstructed so that teachers will not be forced to teach the Negro child sixty ways to despise himself, and thereby perpetuate his false sense of inferiority, and the white child 134 ways to adore himself, and thereby perpetuate his false sense of superiority.

The tendency to ignore the Negro's contribution to American life and to strip him of his personhood is as old as the earliest history books and as contemporary as the morning's newspaper. To upset this cultural homicide, the Negro must rise up with an affirmation of his own Olympian manhood. Any movement for the Negro's freedom that overlooks this necessity is only waiting to be buried. As long as the mind is enslaved, the body can never be free. Psychological freedom, a firm sense of self-esteem, is the most powerful weapon against the long night of physical slavery. No Lincolnian emancipation proclamation or Johnsonian civil rights bill can totally bring this kind of freedom. The Negro will only be free when he reaches down to the inner depths of his own being and signs with the pen and ink of assertive manhood his own emancipation proclamation. And, with a spirit straining toward true self-esteem, the Negro must boldly throw off the manacles of self-abegnation and say to himself and to the world, "I am somebody. I am a person. I am a man with dignity and honor. I have a rich and noble history. How painful and exploited that history has been. Yes, I was a slave through my foreparents and I am not ashamed of that. I'm ashamed of the people who were so sinful to make me a slave." Yes, we must stand up and say, "I'm black and I'm beautiful," and this self-affirmation is the black man's need, made compelling by the white man's crimes against him.

Another basic challenge is to discover how to organize our strength in terms of economic and political power. No one can deny that the Negro is in dire need of this kind of legitimate power. Indeed, one of the great problems that the Negro confronts is his lack of power. From old plantations of the South to newer ghettos of the North, the Negro has been confined to a life of voicelessness and powerlessness. Stripped of the right to make decisions concerning his life and destiny he has been subject to the authoritarian and sometimes whimsical decisions of this white power structure. The plantation and ghetto were created by those who had power, both to confine those who had no power and to perpetuate their powerlessness. The problem of transforming the ghetto, therefore, is a problem of power—confrontation of the forces of power demanding change and the forces of power dedicated to the preserving of the status quo. Now power properly understood is nothing but the ability to achieve purpose. It is the strength required to bring about social, political and economic change. Walter Reuther defined power one day. He said, "Power is the ability of a labor union like the UAW to make the most powerful corporation in the world, General Motors, say, 'Yes' when it wants to say 'No.' That's power."

Now a lot of us are preachers, and all of us have our moral convictions and concerns, and so often have problems with power. There is nothing wrong with power if power is used correctly. You see, what happened is that some of our philosophers got off base. And one of the great problems of history is that the concepts of love and power have usually been contrasted as opposites—polar opposites—so that love is identified with a resignation of power, and power with a denial of love.

It was this misinterpretation that caused Nietzsche, who was a philosopher of the will to power, to reject the Christian concept of love. It was this same misinterpretation which induced Christian theologians to reject the Nietzschean philosophy of the will to power in the name of the Christian idea of love. Now, we've got to get this thing right. What is needed is a realization that power without love is reckless and abusive, and love without power is sentimental and anemic. Power at its best is love implementing the demands of justice, and justice at its best is power correcting everything that stands against love. And this is what we must see as we move on. What has happened is that we have had it wrong and confused in our own country, and this has led Negro Americans in the past to seek their goals through power devoid of love and conscience.

This is leading a few extremists today to advocate for Negroes the same destructive and conscienceless power that they have justly abhorred in whites. It is precisely this collision of immoral power with powerless morality which constitutes the major crisis of our times.

We must develop a program that will drive the nation to a guaranteed annual income. Now, early in this century this proposal would have been greeted with ridicule and denunciation, as destructive of initiative and responsibility. At that time economic status was considered the measure of the individual's ability and talents. And, in the thinking of that day, the absence of worldly goods indicated a want of industrious habits and moral fiber. We've come a long way in our understanding of human motivation and of the blind operation of our economic system. Now we realize that dislocations in the market operations of our economy and the prevalence of discrimination thrust people into idleness and bind them in constant or frequent unemployment against their will. Today the poor are less often dismissed, I hope, from our consciences by being branded as inferior or incompetent. We also know that no matter how dynamically the economy develops and expands, it does not eliminate all poverty.

The problem indicates that our emphasis must be twofold. We must create full employment or we must create incomes. People must be made consumers by one method or the other. Once they are placed in this position we need to be concerned that the potential of the individual is not wasted. New forms of work that enhance the social good will have to be devised for those for whom traditional jobs are not available. In 1879 Henry George anticipated this state of affairs when he wrote in *Progress and Poverty*:

> The fact is that the work which improves the condition of mankind, the work which extends knowledge and increases power and enriches literature and elevates thought, is not done to secure a living. It is not the work of slaves driven to their tasks either by the task, by the taskmaster, or by animal necessity. It is the work of men who somehow find a form of work that brings a security for its own sake and a state of society where want is abolished.

Work of this sort could be enormously increased, and we are likely to find that the problems of housing and education, instead of preceding the elimination of poverty, will themselves be affected if poverty is first abolished. The poor transformed into purchasers will do a great deal on their own to alter housing decay. Negroes who have a double disability will have a greater effect on discrimination when they have the additional weapon of cash to use in their struggle.

Beyond these advantages, a host of positive psychological changes inevitably will result from widespread economic security. The dignity of the individual will flourish when the decisions concerning his life are in his own hands, when he has the means to seek self-improvement. Personal conflicts among husbands, wives and children will diminish when the unjust measurement of human worth on the scale of dollars is eliminated.

Now our country can do this. John Kenneth Galbraith said that a guaranteed annual income could be done for about twenty billion dollars a year. And I say to you today, that if our nation can spend thirty-five billion dollars a year to fight an unjust, evil war in Vietnam, and twenty billion dollars to put a man on the moon, it can spend billions of dollars to put God's children on their own two feet right here on earth.

Now, let me say briefly that we must reaffirm our commitment to nonviolence. I want to stress this. The futility of violence in the struggle for racial justice has been tragically etched in all the recent Negro riots. Yesterday, I tried to analyze the riots and deal with their causes. Today I want to give the other side. There is certainly something painfully sad about a riot. One sees screaming youngsters and angry adults fighting hopelessly and aimlessly against impossible odds. And deep down within them, you can see a desire for self-destruction, a kind of suicidal longing.

Occasionally Negroes contend that the 1965 Watts riot and the other riots in various cities represented effective civil rights action. But those who express this view always end up with stumbling words when asked what concrete gains have been won as a result. At best, the riots have produced a little additional antipoverty money allotted by frightened government officials, and a few water-sprinklers to cool the children of the ghettos. It is something like improving the food in the prison while the people remain securely incarcerated behind bars. Nowhere have the riots won any concrete improvement such as have the organized protest demonstrations. When one tries to pin down advocates of violence as to what acts would be effective, the answers are blatantly illogical. Sometimes they talk of overthrowing racist state and local governments and they talk about guerrilla warfare. They fail to see that no internal revolution has ever succeeded in overthrowing a government by violence unless the government had already lost the allegiance and effective control of its armed forces. Anyone in his right mind knows that this will not happen in the United States. In a violent racial situation, the power structure has the local police, the state troopers, the National Guard and, finally, the army to call on—all of which are predominantly white. Furthermore, few if any violent revolutions have been successful unless the violent minority had the sympathy and support of the nonresistant majority. Castro may have had only a few Cubans actually fighting with him up in the hills, but he could never have overthrown the Batista regime unless he had the sympathy of the vast majority of Cuban people.

It is perfectly clear that a violent revolution on the part of American blacks would find no sympathy and support from the white population and very little from the majority of the Negroes themselves. This is no time for romantic illusions and empty philosophical debates about freedom. This is a time for action. What is needed is a strategy for change, a tactical program that will bring the Negro into the mainstream of American life as quickly as possible. So far, this has only been offered by the nonviolent movement. Without recognizing this we will end up with solutions that don't solve, answers that don't answer and explanations that don't explain.

And so I say to you today that I still stand by nonviolence. And I am still convinced that it is the most potent weapon available to the Negro in his struggle for justice in this country. And the other thing is that I am concerned about a better world. I'm concerned about justice. I'm concerned about brotherhood. I'm concerned about truth. And when one is concerned about these, he can never advocate violence. For through violence you may murder a murderer but you can't murder murder. Through violence you may murder a liar but you can't establish truth. Through violence you may murder a hater, but you can't murder hate. Darkness cannot put out darkness. Only light can do that.

And I say to you, I have also decided to stick to love. For I know that love is ultimately the only answer to mankind's problems. And I'm going to talk about it everywhere I go. I know it isn't popular to talk about it in some circles today. I'm not talking about emotional bosh when I talk about love, I'm talking about a strong, demanding love. And I have seen too much hate. I've seen too much hate on the faces of sheriffs in the South. I've seen hate on the faces of too many Klansmen and too many White Citizens Councilors in the South to want to hate myself, because every time I see it, I know that it does something to their faces and their personalities and I say to myself that hate is too great a burden to bear. I have decided to love. If you are seeking the highest good, I think you can find it through love. And the beautiful thing is that we are moving against wrong when we do it, because John was right, God is love. He who hates does not know God, but he who has love has the key that unlocks the door to the meaning of ultimate reality.

I want to say to you as I move to my conclusion, as we talk about "Where do we go from here," that we honestly face the fact that the movement must address itself to the question of restructuring the whole of American society. There are forty million poor people here. And one day we must ask the question, "Why are there forty million poor people in America?" And when you begin to ask that question, you are raising questions about the economic system, about a broader distribution of wealth. When you ask that question, you begin to question the capitalistic economy. And I'm simply saying that more and more, we've got to begin to ask questions about the whole society. We are called upon to help the discouraged beggars in life's marketplace. But one day we must come to see that an edifice which produces beggars needs restructuring. It means that questions must be raised. You see, my friends, when you deal with this, you begin to ask the question, "Who owns the oil?" You begin to ask the question, "Who owns the iron ore?" You begin to ask the question, "Why is it that people have to pay water bills in a world that is two-thirds water?" These are questions that must be asked.

Now, don't think that you have me in a "bind" today. I'm not talking about communism.

What I'm saying to you this morning is that communism forgets that life is individual. Capitalism forgets that life is social, and the kingdom of brotherhood is found neither in the thesis of communism nor the antithesis of capitalism but in a higher synthesis. It is found in a higher synthesis that combines the truths of both. Now, when I say question the whole society, it means ultimately coming to see that the problem of racism, the problem of economic exploitation, and the problem of war are all tied together. These are the triple evils that are interrelated.

If you will let me be a preacher just a little bit—One night, a juror came to Jesus and he wanted to know what he could do to be saved.

Jesus didn't get bogged down in the kind of isolated approach of what he shouldn't do. Jesus didn't say, "Now Nicodemus, you must stop lying." He didn't say, "Nicodemus, you must stop cheating if you are doing that." He didn't say, "Nicodemus, you must not commit adultery." He didn't say, "Nicodemus, now you must stop drinking liquor if you are doing that excessively." He said something altogether different, because Jesus realized something basic—that if a man will lie, he will steal. And if a man will steal, he will kill. So instead of just getting bogged down in one thing, Jesus looked at him and said, "Nicodemus, you must be born again."

He said, in other words, "Your whole structure must be changed." A nation that will keep people in slavery for 244 years will "thingify" them—make them things. Therefore they will exploit them, and poor people generally, economically. And a nation that will exploit economically will have to have foreign investments and everything else, and will have to use its military might to protect them. All of these problems are tied together. What I am saying today is that we must go from this convention and say, "America, you must be born again!"

So, I conclude by saying again today that we have a task and let us go out with a "divine dissatisfaction." Let us be dissatisfied until America will no longer have a high blood pressure of creeds and an anemia of deeds. Let us be dissatisfied until the tragic walls that separate the outer city of wealth and comfort and the inner city of poverty and despair shall be crushed by the battering rams of the forces of justice. Let us be dissatisfied until those that live on the outskirts of hope are brought into the metropolis of daily security. Let us be dissatisfied until slums are cast into the junk heaps of history, and every family is living in a decent sanitary home. Let us be dissatisfied until the dark yesterdays of segregated schools will be transformed into bright tomorrows of quality, integrated education. Let us be dissatisfied until integration is not seen as a problem but as an opportunity to participate in the beauty of diversity. Let us be dissatisfied until men and women, however black they may be, will be judged on the basis of the content of their character and not on the basis of the color of their skin. Let us be dissatisfied. Let us be dissatisfied until every state capitol houses a governor who will do justly, who will love mercy and who will walk humbly with his God. Let us be dissatisfied until from every city hall, justice will roll, down like waters and righteousness like a mighty stream. Let us be dissatisfied until that day when the lion and the lamb shall lie down together, and every man will sit under his own vine and fig tree and none shall be afraid. Let us be dissatisfied. And men will recognize that out of one blood God made all men to dwell upon the face of the earth. Let us be dissatisfied until that day when nobody will shout "White Power!"—when nobody will shout "Black Power!"—but everybody will talk about God's power and human power.

I must confess, my friends, the road ahead will not always be smooth. There will be still rocky places of frustration and meandering points of bewilderment. There will be inevitable setbacks here and there. There will be those moments when the buoyancy of hope will be transformed into the fatigue of despair. Our dreams will sometimes be shattered and our ethereal hopes blasted. We may again with tear-drenched eyes have to stand before the bier of some courageous civil rights worker whose life will be snuffed out by the dastardly acts of bloodthirsty mobs. Difficult and painful as it is, we must walk on in the days ahead with an audacious faith in the future. And as we continue our charted course, we may gain consolation in the words so nobly left by that great black bard who was also a great freedom fighter of yesterday, James Weldon Johnson:

> Stony the road we trod,
> Bitter the chastening rod
> Felt in the days
> When hope unborn had died.
>
> Yet with a steady beat,
> Have not our weary feet
> Come to the place
> For which our fathers sighed?
>
> We have come over the way
> That with tears hath been watered.
> We have come treading our paths
> Through the blood of the slaughtered,
>
> Out from the gloomy past,
> Till now we stand at last
> Where the bright gleam
> Of our bright star is cast.

Let this affirmation be our ringing cry. It will give us the courage to face the uncertainties of the future. It will give our tired feet new strength as we continue our forward stride toward the city of freedom. When our days become dreary with low-hovering clouds of despair, and when our nights become darker than a thousand midnights, let us remember that there is a creative force in this universe, working to pull down the gigantic mountains of evil, a power that is able to make a way out of no way and transform dark yesterdays into bright tomorrows. Let us realize the arc of the moral universe is long but it bends toward justice.

Let us realize that William Cullen Bryant is right: "Truth crushed to earth will rise again." Let us go out realizing that the Bible is right: "Be not deceived, God is not mocked. Whatsoever a man soweth, that shall he also reap." This is for hope for the future, and with this faith we will be able to sing in some not too distant tomorrow with a cosmic past tense, "We have overcome, we have overcome, deep in my heart, I did believe we would overcome."

DISCUSSION QUESTIONS

1. Why did King continue to support nonviolence?
2. King talks about power and love as solutions to deep-seated problems. How do you reconcile the two concepts?

DEBATING THE CIVIL RIGHTS MOVEMENT: THE VIEW FROM THE TRENCHES

Charles Payne

W hich of the following offers the best interpretation of the civil rights movement?

A. The American South had a long tradition of racial oppression, but during the civil rights movement, the weight of American institutions—the presidency, the judicial system, the media, the American sense of fair play—were finally brought to bear on the problem, leading to remarkable changes in southern race relations.

B. Far from being the solution, American institutions have always played important roles in the creation and maintenance of racism. What happened in the movement was that civil rights activists were able to maneuver around those institutions to alleviate some of the system's worst features.

Which strikes you as the better summary? Mind you, people who participated in the movement would have a wide range of interpretations. How, then, can you know? What information are you drawing on when you make your choice? Where does that information come from? Of all the possible historical viewpoints, which ones are most likely to have been preserved in the information to which you have access? Which have been slighted? With what consequences?

We could and should ask these questions about any significant historical phenomenon, but it may be especially important to understand

115

how they apply to the "history" of the civil rights movement. The way we think about that period continues to shape how we think about race relations in our time and how we think about the larger problem of creating a more just society.

FROM WORLD WAR II THROUGH THE 1950s

But in this age, time is short, even for the young.
The sands run fast.

Ralph J. Bunche, commencement address,
Fisk University, May 30, 1949

In 1929, Charles Hamilton Houston—Phi Beta Kappa at Amherst, first Black man to serve on the *Harvard Law Review*—became dean of Howard University's Law School and immediately set about making it an instrument of struggle. A lawyer, he liked to say, is either a social engineer or parasite. He fired faculty who did not meet his standards and flunked out students in droves. Thurgood Marshall entered Howard Law in 1930 with a class of thirty. Only eight or ten lasted to graduation. Houston's motto was "No tea for the feeble, no crepe for the dead." The legal talent that made possible a string of pro–civil rights Supreme Court decisions in the 1930s and 1940s, culminating in *Brown v. Board of Education* in 1954, was nurtured (if that is the word for what they went through) largely at Howard Law.

Brown was more than a legal battle. It was one element in a decades-long struggle for equity in education, a struggle that required Blacks in local communities across the South to expose themselves to physical violence and economic repression. In 1947 the Blacks of Clarendon County, South Carolina, for example, decided to ask the school superintendent for a bus for their children. In a pattern that would be repeated many times—Blacks ask for small adjustments in the system, the authorities refuse, Blacks then make more radical demands—the superintendent refused, and the Black community decided to launch a fight for the complete equalization of schools. The leaders of the Clarendon County movement expected trouble; you could not attack white supremacy in South Carolina and not expect trouble. They had not, however, fully considered the number of weapons the system could bring to bear. The man they chose to lead them was a Methodist minister, J. A. Delaine, and he caught nearly the full weight of the repression. In his history of *Brown,* Richard Kluger says of Delaine:

> Before it was over, they fired him from the little schoolhouse at which he had taught devotedly for ten years. And they fired his wife and two of his sisters and a niece. And they threatened him with bodily harm. And they sued him on trumped up charges and convicted him in a kangaroo court and left with a judgement that denied him credit from any bank. And they burned his house to the ground while the fire department stood around watching the flames consume the night. And they stoned the church at which he pastored. And fired shotguns at him out of the dark. But he was not Job, and so he fired back and called the police, who did not come and kept not coming. Then he fled, driving north at eighty-five miles an hour over country roads, until he was across the state line. Soon after, they burned his church to the ground and charged him, for having shot back that night, with felonious assault with a deadly weapon, and so he became an official fugitive from justice.

Similar stories were being repeated across the South between the mid-1940s and the late 1950s. In the wake of World War II, Black activists were more aggressive, to which the white South responded with a wave of repression. Not all of those who got caught by it were men. Like Delaine, Septima Clark lost her career because of her social activism. Born around the turn of the century, the daughter of a cook and a washerwoman, Clark became a schoolteacher in the area around Charleston, South Carolina. After World War I, she became involved in a fight to get Black teachers and principals hired in Charleston. Following years brought other battles—to equalize pay between white and Black teachers, to get more funding for Black schools and a longer school year. By the mid-1950s, she was deeply involved in the state branch of the National Association for the Advancement of Colored People (NAACP) when the state declared the organization subversive and forbade any state or city employee to be a member. Clark refused to deny her membership and was immediately fired.

Fortunately, the year before, she had begun attending classes at the Highlander Folk School in Tennessee. Started during the Depression, Highlander was among the most unique institutions in the South. One of its founders was Myles Horton, who had grown up in a family of poor white Tennessee sharecroppers. He saw Highlander as a school for the poor of Appalachia, a school where the curriculum was essentially about activism, a place where coal miners, steel workers, mill workers, and others could come to learn how to organize. From its inception, it was also a place concerned with attacking white supremacy, a place where civil rights workers could find training and support. Few significant southern civil rights activists in the 1940s and 1950s did not have some contact with Highlander. It was at Highlander that "We Shall Overcome" was introduced to the movement. No matter what people came there for, Highlander insisted—in contradiction to Tennessee law and southern custom—on interracial living, a philosophy that initially discomfited Black visitors just as much as white ones. Visitor after visitor testified that the experience of egalitarian living in an interracial situation had greater impact on them than the courses and workshops.

Already an experienced activist when she first came to Highlander, Clark found the school a supportive, stimulating environment. She started bringing friends to workshops there and then running workshops herself. When she was fired, Highlander made her its director of education, a position from which she was able to refine Highlander's distinctive style of work. Highlander was founded on a philosophy of struggle that was an alternative to the legal gradualism of the NAACP, on the one hand, or to Dr. Martin Luther King's charisma, on the other. Rather, Highlander espoused a form of participatory democracy. Its statement of purpose, drafted by Clark, speaks of "broadening the scope of democracy to include everyone and deepening the concept to include every relationship." In practical terms, that meant that Highlander wanted to identify and groom leadership at the local level, not just provide it from the outside.

Nothing better illustrates the Highlander style than the Citizenship Schools that Clark developed. She had only been on staff a few months when one of her old students came to her for help. He had just lost an election for school board on Johns Island, one of the Sea Islands opposite Charleston. Blacks made up a large majority of the population, but only a few were able to navigate through the various obstacles the state used to prevent Blacks from voting. This situation was all the more complicated because most Black adults could neither read nor write. Clark, whose first teaching job had been on Johns, developed a program for teaching adults to read and write and then to register, which entailed being able to interpret a section of the state constitution to the satisfaction of the local registrar.

The first class, the existence of which was carefully hidden from whites on the island, had fourteen students, eleven of whom were able to register. From those modest beginnings, the Citizenship Schools grew into one of the most important civil rights initiatives of the late 1950s and early 1960s. Nearly ten thousand people would be trained as teachers and as many as two hundred schools would be in operation at one time "in people's kitchens, in beauty parlors and under trees in the summertime." Across the South, Citizenship Schools and teachers provided much of the on-ground leadership for other civil rights organizations.

This was very much in keeping with how Septima Clark saw the schools. Voting was not, for her, so much an end in itself as it was an organizing device. "The basic purpose of the Citizenship Schools," she wrote, "is discovering local community leaders. . . . It is my belief that creative leadership is present in any community and only awaits discovery and development." For some in the movement, finding and grooming leadership, transforming individuals, was as important as winning legislative victories, perhaps more so in the long run. Political victories are transitory; the powers that be can grant them today and withdraw them tomorrow unless the movement has created people who are always capable of fighting for themselves. Ella Baker certainly thought so. For her, the movement could not be something in which a few big leaders were going to lead the singing masses to freedom. People, she thought, had to learn to lead themselves.

> My basic sense of it has always been to get people to understand that in the long run they themselves are the only protection they have against violence or injustice. . . . People have to be made to understand that they cannot look for salvation anywhere but to themselves.

If one thinks of the movement that way, powerful oratory and big demonstrations may not be important, may even be counterproductive, unless they contribute to the goal of developing a broad leadership base. She was no fan of centralized, charismatic leadership precisely because of its antidemocratic tendencies.

I have always felt it was a handicap for oppressed people to depend so largely on a leader, because unfortunately in our culture, the charismatic leader usually becomes a leader because he has found a spot in the public limelight. It usually means that the media made him, and the media may undo him.

What we need, she argued, is people "who are interested not in being leaders as much as in developing leadership in others." If you can give them the light, people can find their own way. That meant you could not just lead people to change. They had to be a part of the work themselves. She would have agreed emphatically with what James Farmer of the Congress of Racial Equality (CORE) said about the need

> to involve the people themselves, individually, personally, in the struggle for their own freedom. Not simply because it was clear that no one else was going to confer liberty upon them, but because in the very act of working for the impersonal cause of racial freedom, a man experiences, almost like grace, a large measure of private freedom. Or call it a new comprehension of his own identity, an intuition of the expanding boundaries of his self, which, if not the same thing as freedom, is its radical source.

Baker came into the 1960s with more than three decades of activist experience. A product of rural North Carolina, by the Depression she was in Harlem teaching Black history and organizing domestic workers, economic cooperatives, and adult education programs. In one job application she noted that she had maintained at least a speaking acquaintance with the leaders of "the articulate mass and semi-mass movements" in the area. The application was for a position with the NAACP, the most important civil rights organization of the period. From 1941, she was an assistant field secretary, which meant spending half the year traveling through the South, organizing new branches and advising established ones. That eventually led to a position as national director of branches, a position she held during the organization's most dynamic period of growth.

She brought her distinctive philosophy to the position, which meant she had her misgivings about the organization for which she was working. The NAACP, she thought, was overly committed to a legal strategy that left most of its membership—four hundred thousand by

1944—little meaningful role in the development of policy and program. Like many of the leaders with whom she had worked in the Deep South, she was increasingly impatient with the organization's conservatism. The leadership was putting too much energy into worrying about how much recognition they were getting from important white people, a concern that helped prevent the organization from taking a confrontational stance even when that would have made tactical sense. The program was overly middle-class, not strong enough on the kinds of economic issues that meant most to working-class Black people. Perhaps above all, she found the organization too centralized; too many decisions were being made in New York. The annual conventions were carefully staged exercises in pseudodemocracy. The national staff was really calling the shots.

She wanted to use her position as director of branches to open the organization up somewhat. She tried to have more decisions made in the branches rather than in New York, and she was able to establish a training program for local leaders. By 1946, she decided that democratizing the NAACP was beyond even her considerable talents, and she resigned, working for a variety of causes over the next decade.

When the Southern Christian Leadership Conference (SCLC) was founded in 1957, it actually represented an alliance across generations of activists. The face that public saw was that of the Reverend King, but in fact he was twenty-eight years old and politically inexperienced. A cadre of older activists formed around him to give him support, including Bayard Rustin, a longtime labor, peace, and civil rights activist, and Stanley Levison, a Jewish lawyer with much experience in left and radical causes. They were able to talk Ella Baker into going south once more where she eventually became the SCLC's first full-time executive director. She was the ideal choice for a fledgling organization in that she had such extensive networks among southern activists. On the other hand, she was an outspoken woman in an organization that did not expect or appreciate that attitude from women; she was suspicious of charismatic leadership in an organization that was built on it, was impatient with ministerial conservatism, and did not personally believe in the nonviolence the organization was espousing. Her years at SCLC were tense, but when the sit-ins erupted in 1960, she was in a position to help channel that energy into an organization that became a model for American activists of all types.

During the 1940s, when Baker was bemoaning the conservatism of the NAACP, one of the most significant alternatives to it was provided by A. Philip Randolph. Formerly the editor of an important African-American socialist magazine, in 1925 he organized the Brotherhood of Sleeping Car Porters, the most important Black union of its day. The presidency of the union gave him a pulpit from which he gave eloquent voice to the concerns of Black workers for four decades. As befits a man with union roots, he was not much given to the moral suasion and legal gradualism in which the NAACP specialized. His style was to threaten, to embarrass, to put the masses into the street. When it became clear that World War II defense industries were excluding Blacks, Randolph, to the dismay of more timid Black leadership, threatened to march a hundred thousand protesting Negroes on Washington unless President Franklin D. Roosevelt did something. He was criticized for keeping the March on Washington Movement all-Black, but he was adamant about that. "You take ten thousand dollars from a white man," he said, "you've got his ten thousand dollars but he's got your movement." His thinking also echoed Ella Baker's in how it balanced concern for immediate tactical objectives with concern for larger questions about how the race was developing. In order for a people to develop, they had to fight for their own causes, not have friends do their fighting for them. Sympathetic whites could best help through their own organizations (a position the Black Panthers would revive a quarter-century later).

After the war, Randolph played a role in President Harry Truman's decision to desegregate the armed forces. In 1948, amid cries of treason, Randolph promised that if the services were not desegregated, he would lead a campaign of massive civil disobedience modeled after Gandhi's approach, and he pledged to "openly counsel, aid and abet youth, both white and Negro, to quarantine any jimcrow conscription system." Randolph pushed Truman so that in one meeting the president virtually threw him out of his office. Much established Black leadership, including the NAACP, thought Randolph had gone too far, but 70 percent of young Black men polled in Harlem agreed with Randolph.

In terms of brass, at least, Birmingham's Fred Shuttlesworth was a worthy match for Randolph. In its attempt to harass the NAACP, Alabama went South Carolina one better. South Carolina merely decided that public employees could not be members of the NAACP; in 1956, Alabama declared the organization illegal. NAACP members immediately reconstituted themselves as the Alabama Christian Movement for Human Rights (ACMHR), which proceeded to give white Alabama even more trouble than had the NAACP. While the NAACP restricted itself mostly to filing lawsuits, the ACMHR, with Shuttlesworth as president, was willing to engage in boycotts, pickets, and demonstrations. When the Supreme Court decided, in December 1956, that bus segregation in Montgomery was unconstitutional, the ACMHR decided to protest Birmingham's segregated buses. Black people had nicknamed Birmingham "Bombingham" and for very good reason. The night before the protest was to begin, the Shuttlesworth home was bombed, injuring a visiting deacon and two of the Shuttlesworth children, though Shuttlesworth himself was untouched. "I wasn't saved to run," he announced.

That kind of hard-headed determination frightened more traditional Black leaders, but it also inspired some people. Shuttlesworth got death threats constantly, the police harassed him in every way they could, including wiretaps, and both the police and the Ku Klux Klan (in Birmingham, it was hard to tell the two apart) harassed his followers. In 1957, in the wake of the Little Rock Crisis, Shuttlesworth was leading four Black youngsters, including two of his own children, to register at the white high school when he was attacked by a mob and beaten with brass knuckles and bicycle chains. His wife was stabbed. The following spring, there was another attempt to bomb his church. Nonetheless, for the rest of the decade, Shuttlesworth and his followers attacked white supremacy in Birmingham—pushing the city to hire Black police officers, open parks and libraries to Negroes, desegregate its schools, and allow Blacks to vote.

That Shuttlesworth survived the 1950s is a small miracle. Others were less fortunate. Harry T. Moore of Mims, Florida, was a schoolteacher, often described as a shy man. Nonetheless, he was staunch enough in his politics. The work that he was known for and that had propelled him to the presidency of the state NAACP was his persistent agitation for the equalization of the educational resources given to Black and white youngsters. In 1951, he campaigned for the prosecution of a sheriff who had shot two Negro youths, killing one. Shortly after he and his wife had retired on Christmas Eve that year, a bomb destroyed their bedroom. He died immediately and his wife a few days later.

In the prewar years, southern Blacks typically laid low after a racial killing. It was a sign of changing times that Blacks from across the state packed his funeral, paying homage to a man who was for them the kind of symbol of persistence and integrity that Medgar Evers would become for Blacks in Mississippi. The Black press saw another sign of change in the fact that the murder was one of a wave of bombings across the South in the early 1950s. The fact that the most dangerous defenders of racism were hiding behind bombs in the night rather than rallying lynch mobs in the open suggested that killers saw a need to be more cautious. It was a measure of progress, however grim.

When Americans speak of the "civil rights movement," they are un-likely to be thinking of Harry T. Moore or A. Philip Randolph, Septima Clark, Ella Baker, J. A. Delaine, Charles Hamilton Houston, or Fred Shuttlesworth. They and the struggles they represent are not a part of American history as it is normally taught, with its streamlined, homoge-nized version of the movement. Saying that most Americans have been raised on a whitewashed version of movement history is more than a bad pun.

What difference does it make if we leave people like this out? At the very least, it means that we lose touch with the complexity of the historical process. All kinds of people are important to this history— Appalachian whites, Black professionals from quite privileged back-grounds, quasi socialists, radical democrats, church-based activists, advocates of self-defense for Black people, advocates of racial separatism, people as concerned with human development as with legislative victories, people who saw education, the need for self-affirmation, access to jobs, and access to the political system as intertwined. It is not a history that can be comprehended in terms of a couple of dominant figures or any one form of politics, and it is not at all clear that it can be well understood in terms of "civil rights."

To paraphrase Julian Bond of the Student Nonviolent Coordinating Committee (SNCC), American popular and academic culture has been permeated by a master narrative about the movement. The narrative goes something like this:

> Traditionally, relationships between the races in the South were op-pressive. In the 1954, the Supreme Court decided this was wrong. Inspired by the court, courageous Americans, Black and white, took protest to the street, in the form of sit-ins, bus boycotts, and freedom

rides. The protest movement, led by the brilliant and eloquent Dr. Martin Luther King, aided by a sympathetic federal government, most notably the Kennedy brothers and a born-again Lyndon Johnson, was able to make America understand racial discrimination as a moral issue. Once Americans understood that discrimination was wrong, they quickly moved to remove racial prejudice and discrimination from American life, as evidenced by the Civil Rights Acts of 1964 and 1965. Dr. King was tragically slain in 1968. Fortunately, by that time the country had been changed, changed for the better in some fundamental ways. The movement was a remarkable victory for all Americans. By the 1970s, southern states where Blacks could not have voted ten years earlier were sending African Americans to Congress. Inexplicably, just as the civil rights victories were piling up, many Black Americans, under the banner of Black Power, turned their backs on American society.

In its concentration on national institutions and leaders, on discrimination as a moral issue, on the period between the mid-1950s and the mid-1960s, in its restriction of leadership roles to elite men, on interracial cooperation, in its treatment of the movement as a great victory and of radicalism as irrational, the narrative reflects the typical assumptions of what might be called the naive, top-down, normative perspective on movement history. More recently, scholars have been calling for a reconsideration of the traditional narrative. They have raised a number of points:

1. Placing so much emphasis on national leadership and national institutions minimizes the importance of local struggle and makes it difficult to appreciate the role "ordinary" people played in changing the country and the enormous personal costs that sometimes entailed for them. It implicitly creates the impression that historical dynamism resides among elites—usually white, usually male, usually educated—and that nonelites lack historical agency. The gender bias of traditional history is especially inappropriate in this case in that we know that at the local level, women provided a disproportionate share of the leadership in the early 1960s.
2. Normative social analysis is analysis that emphasizes the primacy of norms and values in shaping the behaviors of individuals or

groups. In the master narrative, it shows up in the emphasis on the morality of national leadership, on the church, legal institutions, and interracalism. The movement gets reduced to a "protest" movement. African-American activism is sometimes equated with the church, the most normative of institutions. The danger is that this emphasis may oversimplify the motives of actors, understating the salience of disruption, of economic and political pressure. The emphasis on the normative character of the civil rights movement is in considerable contrast to the way other movements are portrayed. When we think about the labor movement, for example, we are a good deal less likely to invoke normative explanations. We see that as a struggle over privilege, although each side tried to wrap its cause in the mantle of higher morality.

3. A top-down perspective can lose any sense of the complexity of the African-American community—its class, gender, cultural, regional, and ideological divisions—and how that complexity shaped responses to oppression. One gets a few well-defined leaders and then the undifferentiated masses.

4. Concentration on the period between the mid-1950s and the mid-1960s—the Montgomery to Memphis framework—underplays the salience of earlier periods of struggle. All apart from their significance for understanding the modern civil rights movement, those earlier periods of struggle are important in their own right as one of the keys to understanding the evolving self-consciousness of African Americans and the shifting constraints that confronted them.

5. A top-down perspective presumes that the most appropriate historical markers have to do with legislative/policy changes. This position makes it very difficult to understand the movement as a transforming experience for individuals or as an evolving culture, which in turn makes it very difficult to understand the radicalization of the movement.

6. A top-down perspective typically implies that the movement can be understood solely through large-scale, dramatic events, thus obscuring the actual social infrastructure that sustained the movement on a day-to-day basis.

It is not an either/or choice. Scholars advocating a more bottom-up approach are not denying the critical importance of national institutions, but they are contending that traditional top-down scholarship has tended to focus on them so exclusively as to make it impossible to understand just how complex the movement really was and how varied the sources of its dynamism were. To understand that, we need more sophisticated work from a variety of perspectives.

By way of example of illustrating a less sophisticated top-down approach, we can look at how the Montgomery bus boycott, perhaps our most familiar origin myth about the movement, is normally presented. What we are usually told is that a tired woman refused to give up her seat on the bus and an eloquent, nonviolent prophet rose up to lead the grateful masses, and the Supreme Court eventually saw the justness of their cause. That rendering hides more than it reveals.

For one thing, the traditional story obscures the fact that the people who made the boycott happen had long activist backgrounds, including the venerable E. D. Nixon, a pullman porter with a sixth-grade education, in his mid-fifties at the time of the boycott and probably the most influential Black man in town, at least in the eyes of the Black masses. Nixon had organized the state branch of the Brotherhood of Sleeping Car Porters in 1928. He attributed much of what he had learned about organizing to A. Philip Randolph, the founder of the Brotherhood. In the 1930s Nixon, along with Myles Horton at Highlander, tried to organize Alabama farm laborers, and he organized a committee to make sure that Alabama Blacks got their fair share of benefits from federal programs. In 1940, he helped organize the Montgomery Voters League; in 1944, he led a march of 750 people on the registrar's office; from 1939 to 1951, he headed the Montgomery NAACP; and from 1951 to 1953, the state conference.

The portrait of Rosa Parks as some simple woman who accidentally got caught up in great historical events is a complete distortion. She had spent her adult life looking for a way to make a difference. In 1943, she joined the NAACP under Nixon, became its secretary, and worked in voter registration campaigns; she first registered herself in 1945. She also ran the local NAACP Youth Council and served as secretary to the state NAACP Conference of Branches. She had attended one of Ella Baker's Leadership Training Conferences in the 1940s and had spent a week at the Highlander Folk School in 1955. From the 1940s on, she had refused on several occasions to comply with bus segregation laws, frequently enough that some bus drivers recognized her on sight and simply refused to stop for her. King's comment about her—"She was tracked down by the Zeitgeist—the spirit of the times"—is precisely wrong. She, like Nixon, had spent much of her adult life actively seeking levers of change, not waiting until the times were right.

Jo Ann Robinson was an English professor at nearby Alabama State College and president of the Women's Political Caucus, a group of three hundred educated Black women who had been concerned with voter registration and segregated public facilities since 1946. They had been agitating the city commission about segregated buses since the early 1950s and in May 1954 had sent a letter to the mayor threatening a boycott if improvements were not made. Between the spring of 1955 and the time of the Parks arrest in December, Nixon and the caucus had considered three bus incidents as potential test cases but decided against them on various tactical grounds. The Parks incident gave them the case they wanted.

Nixon and Robinson's group were largely responsible for the initial mobilization of Black Montgomery. Parks was arrested on a Thursday; Nixon started organizing the first meeting of Negro leadership on Friday; by Monday they had organized a boycott that was nearly completely effective among a community of over forty thousand people. That they could mobilize the Black community so thoroughly, so quickly, is a reflection of how well people such as Nixon and Robinson knew their community, knowledge acquired through long years of working in it. When Nixon called the first nineteen ministers, he had to have been making some calculations about which individuals had to be involved to carry the whole of Black Montgomery with them. That knowledge was the product of three decades of meetings, demonstrations, barbershop arguments, and beauty parlor conversations.

What does the background information, even in this sketchy form, add to our understanding of the movement? Potentially, it broadens our conception of leadership, ranging from a woman with a college education to a man whose real education came from union organizing. It leaves an impression of women as thinking, determined activists. It restores a sense of human agency, suggesting, as one scholar put it, "that reflective and purposeful people matter." Montgomery happened because many people worked to make it happen. When we take the high drama of moments such as the boycott out of the longer historical context, we implicitly undervalue the more mundane activities, the sheer persistence that helped make the dramatic breakthroughs possible.

Knowing even a little of the larger story also suggests something about how we might think about King's leadership. In some top-down treatments, of course, King comes to be almost equated with the movement. Fred Poweledge, a journalist who covered the movement, notes:

> In the minds of untold numbers of Americans, for example, the Reverend Dr. Martin Luther King Jr., *was* the civil rights movement. Thought it up, led it, produced its victories, became its sole martyr. Schoolchildren—including Black schoolchildren—are taught this.

In fact, what we see in Montgomery was that King was the inheritor of momentum that other people established, a pattern that was to be repeated often over the next several years. Other people constructed the stage, but once he stepped into the role of movement spokesperson, his charisma, broad appeal, and personal growth allowed him to project the message of the movement in ways that virtually no one could have predicted in 1956.

STUDENT ACTIVISM, DIRECT ACTION, AND THE MORAL DIMENSIONS OF PROTEST

The early 1960s offer a number of illustrations of the complexity of the relationship between King and the larger movement. Montgomery had made him an international figure, but even with the help of the more experienced activists who gathered around him, he found it difficult to translate that capital into a South-wide mass movement. By 1960, SCLC, by its own admission, had made little progress in that regard. For the next two years, as Adam Fairclough puts it in *Martin Luther King, Jr.*, "King found himself being overtaken by events initiated by others."

The sit-ins, starting in February 1960, were first. They were the definitive break with the past, the beginning of a period of sustained mass activism that eventually came to encompass a much broader range of issues than race. From this moment on there is something one can call a "movement" in the South. The wildfire spread of the sit-ins (and the pray-ins, wade-ins, read-ins, etc.) energized civil rights advocates and caught detractors off guard. This was a form of communication for which they had no ready response. Many Americans just assumed that King, the civil rights leader with whom they were most familiar, was behind the new movement and sent money to SCLC intended for the student movement. Actually, his relationship to the sit-ins was marginal. At SNCC's founding conference, the students made a pointed decision not to become a part of SCLC or any other adult organization, a decision encouraged by Ella Baker, who did not want to see this new energy stifled by adult baggage. Even some of the young people who admired King found him a bit too conservative. "De Lawd," some of them called him mockingly. The Atlanta students had to shame him into going on his first sit-in.

Similarly, the freedom rides were a CORE project with a strong assist from SNCC when the original buses were stopped by the violence in Alabama. When King got trapped inside the church with freedom riders in Montgomery, press coverage often centered on King as if the rides were one of his projects. In its attempts to stop the rides, the Kennedy administration often negotiated with King as if that decision were his to make. If it had been his call to make, King would have acquiesced to the Kennedy request for a cooling-off period. It was SNCC and CORE members who insisted that they go on, and they did everything they could to talk him into going with them. His refusal cost him some capital with the kids (and the way he put it—"I think I should choose the time and place of my Golgotha"—struck many of them as the sheerest puffery).

King needed the Albany, Georgia, campaign. SNCC and CORE had seized the initiative with their creative, aggressive tactics. Albany seemed a chance for SCLC to regain some ground. Given his relationships with the other groups, though, that was not going to be easy. The national NAACP, which regarded King as a headline-grabbing, Johnny-come-lately, resented his presence in one of "their" towns and encouraged their people in Albany to keep their distance. At the other end of the ideological spectrum, SNCC organizers, at great danger to themselves, had initiated the Albany Movement and felt a keen sense of ownership. They were less than thrilled to have King coming around to steal their thunder yet again, as it seemed to them. Albany helped solidify

SNCC's critique of King's politics—which, of course, was also its critique of charismatic leadership in general. King, many of them complained, would come into a town where SNCC or CORE had done the dangerous, thankless work of getting something off the ground, give some speeches to the adoring masses and the fawning press, and then fly off to the next place, leaving others to deal with the letdown. King was too cautious, too bourgeois, too concerned about offending the Kennedys. He was a mobilizer, not an organizer, good at involving large numbers of people in short-term, media-oriented events but never in one place long enough to see that a local infrastructure got created that could carry the struggle on with or without him. The actual relationship between King and the young people was probably a good deal more symbiotic than that sounds. Their critique aside, younger activists often needed him to give a boost to flagging local campaigns.

The disagreements between King and the younger activists retained the feel of a family dispute. The fussing and feuding not withstanding, many of them continued to have friendly personal relationships with King, which in part reflects one of the important dimensions of his style, his ability to play the centrist role, to maintain relationships with all the various wings of the movement, to keep himself above much of the organizational and personal rivalry.

The direct action phase of the movement is also an interesting context for thinking about normative interpretations of movement history. To what degree was the movement a movement of moral protest, specifically? To what degree did Americans react to racial inequality as an issue of conscience? In traditional treatments of the movement, the normative emphasis shows up in several ways. One of them is to assert the existence of a post–World War II tendency toward a liberalization of racial attitudes. Hitler's arrogant racism made Americans rethink the homegrown version, the argument goes. Although the general notion of some kind of trend in the direction of more liberal racial attitudes is plausible enough, one wonders what evidence exists for the idea that it was strong enough to affect the course of the movement. How exactly does this liberalization play itself out, public rhetoric aside? Well into the 1960s, civil rights activists were being killed with no chance whatsoever that their murderers could be brought to justice. From the perspective of activists who were dodging bullets, this liberalization must have seemed pretty weak tea indeed. It might also be useful to juxtapose discussions of postwar racial liberalization with discussions of McCarthyism and subsequent Red-baiting. If the confrontation with Hitler made us more aware of the antidemocratic nature of racism, did it also make us more aware of the profoundly antidemocratic tendencies of McCarthyism?

There is no doubt that atrocities such as the bombing deaths of four little girls in Birmingham, the assassination of Medgar Evers, and the murder of civil rights workers including Andrew Goodman, Mickey Schwerner, and James Chaney triggered enormous moral revulsion. Even in those cases, the reaction of the nation seemed more a reaction to the violence used in defense of white supremacy than to white supremacy itself. The lesson of the Albany, Georgia, campaign, which southern white leadership never fully appreciated, was that if the violence could be restrained, ethical and moral issues—to say nothing of constitutional issues—were seldom enough to sustain the nation's attention.

The assumption that the movement was nonviolent contributes greatly to the impression that it was a moral crusade. Nonviolence is the sword that cuts without wounding, as the saying goes. King (who himself was not that steeped in nonviolence when the bus boycott began) explained that nonviolence did not seek to defeat the opponent but to win his friendship and understanding, "to awaken a sense of moral shame in the opponent. The end is redemption and reconciliation." In that philosophical sense, as CORE's James Farmer pointed out in a 1963 essay, the proponents of nonviolence were only a small proportion of the movement's participants. The masses were committed to change, not to particular methods. If nonviolence worked, fine; but if not, they were willing to use other methods.

In 1957, members of the Monroe, North Carolina, NAACP, under the leadership of an ex-serviceman named Robert Williams, engaged in a shoot-out with members of the Klan who were attacking their community. The national NAACP leadership were horrified, but Williams became a hero among much of the rank and file. "We use and approve non-violent resistance," he said. "But we also believe that a man cannot have human dignity if he allows himself to be abused; to be kicked and beaten to the ground, to allow his wife and children to be attacked." As subsequent events would demonstrate, that position probably made a good deal more sense to the average African American—to the average American, period, when he or she was not thinking about race—than talk about redemptive suffering and turning the other cheek. Before it was over, even King would come to question whether nonviolence in its philosophical sense could work in the American context.

Still, young Black activists in the late 1950s and early 1960s saw themselves as appealing to the conscience of the American people. The nation was ultimately on the side of justice and just needed to be prodded. One of the Little Rock Nine refers to watching the troops roll up to Central High beyond those American flags and feeling for the first time that he, too, was an American. The more experience younger activists had dealing with national institutions, the more that kind of confidence in the nation's conscience eroded. Direct action was a two-pronged strategy. It was certainly a moral appeal, but it also meant directly interfering with the life of a community. If people could not respond to the moral dimensions of the problem, they would have to respond to the fact that business as usual was no longer possible. Over time, activists, King included, learned that it was disruption and potential embarrassment that got the national machinery in motion.

The reference to business as usual can be taken literally. Protesters learned quickly that economic interests were among the most important determinants of how people responded to the movement. When southern cities were caught up in demonstrations, they learned, certain elements of the white community tended to be first to want to negotiate an end to them. If the motivations were largely moral, we might expect educators or ministers to be disproportionately represented among those leading their communities out of turmoil. In fact, they were marginal players in most cities. The group most consistently playing the progressive role turns out to have been businesspeople, and their motives were pretty straightforward. Demonstrations were not healthy for the bottom line. Black activists routinely combined sit-ins and demonstrations with boycotts of the downtown merchants. Even when that was not the case, the fear of turmoil tended to keep both Black and white shoppers at home, a de facto boycott. Cash registers fell quiet. In the ensuing silence, southern businesspeople could think a little more clearly; and the more they thought, the more it seemed like they could put up with a little desegregation after all.

Economic pressure was more important than most histories suggest, and so was white fear. King understood that part of his effectiveness was due to the fact that whites were afraid of the alternatives. One student of the Kennedy administration notes that "fear of escalating black militancy and the threat of black violence were indeed among the primary considerations in the administration's key civil rights decisions." By making concessions to moderates, the administration hoped to weaken the position of more radical leaders, some of whom were quite aware of the game being played. After he left the Nation of Islam, Malcolm X was happy to let King and other moderate leaders use him as a bogeyman.

Normative interpretations of the movement are also likely to see the movement as representing a national consensus. Perhaps no one moment symbolizes that better than the March on Washington, Americans of every hue and creed coming together in a coalition of conscience. The backstage realities were more complex, of course. President Kennedy had endorsed the march only very reluctantly, the NAACP thought it questionable, and some of the white speakers threatened to pull out at the last minute because they considered the speech SNCC planned too militant. The administration was still maintaining that it could not protect civil rights workers in the South. In Congress, there were not nearly enough votes to pass the pending civil rights bill. That it passed a year later may have had more to do with Lyndon Johnson's political skill than with any congressional consensus on the merits of the bill.

According to the Gallup polls in the months prior to the march, Congress was well advised to be cautious. Only 49 percent of the public supported a bill to desegregate public accommodations, almost the same percentage who thought the Kennedy administration was pushing civil rights too fast. Seventy-two percent thought it was all right to give federal aid to segregated schools. Sixty percent thought that demonstrations in general were doing more damage to the Negro cause than good; 63 percent thought the March on Washington was a bad idea. Even in 1963, Americans seemed anxious to declare the racial problem solved; 56 percent thought Negroes in their communities were treated the same as whites. Nonetheless, 49 percent thought they might move if a Negro family moved in next door to them, going up to nearly 80 percent if a great number were to move into the neighborhood. The march, which is remembered as a symbol of national unity, actually took place in a nation deeply divided about racial issues, as much then as now.

Normative interpretations of the movement always seem a little self-congratulatory. We Americans, they seem to be saying, ultimately did the right things for the right reasons. We are a moral people. Without debating the merits of that proposition, it is directly at odds with the interpretation many movement participants, even moderates, put on their experience. Uncritical normative interpretations can cause us to lose touch with the evolving consciousness of activists, with the changes in how they understood their world. At the same time that they implicitly understate the extent of the sacrifices made by some of those activists, they can understate the importance of pressure, economic and otherwise, in generating change, and they can create in retrospect a sense of consensus and unity that did not exist at the time.

MISSISSIPPI: THE MIDDLE OF THE ICEBERG

> My fear just finally grew out of me. I had made up my mind. I would die and go to hell before being treated like a dog. I had faith the Almighty would protect me. Right gonna win. But I believe in fighting now; I'll fight in a minute, because you young people haven't saw what I saw in my time. There was a man down here they put in jail, and the KuKlux went down an' shot that man to pieces. I have saw men hung behind cars and drug. I've saw people walk down the Goodman Street an' get push' off and beat to death by white people. And black people stand there lookin' at 'em.
>
> Mr. Robert Cooper Howard, Holmes County

One could wrap the story of the movement in Mississippi around the life of Vernon Dahmer. The owner of a farm, a sawmill, and a grocery store, Dahmer was a leader in efforts to register Black voters in the Hattiesburg area in the early 1950s. In 1953, when he was president of the local NAACP, he sued the sheriff of Forrest County for interfering with Black efforts to vote, an act of great courage. During the 1950s, he tried to interest teenagers in NAACP work, and many of them grew up to be important activists within SNCC or CORE. In the early 1960s, when younger civil rights workers came into the state, he housed them and financed their work. Six months after the passage of the Voting

Rights Act, he went on the radio to say that anybody who was afraid to pay poll tax downtown could pay it at his grocery store; if anybody did not have the money to pay poll tax, he would pay it for them. He and his wife were accustomed to taking turns sitting up at night guarding their home, but during that period they had stopped since they were not being threatened as frequently as had been the case. Their home and grocery store were firebombed that night, apparently by the White Knights of Mississippi, a particularly dangerous branch of the Klan. The house and store were destroyed, and their ten-year-old daughter was badly burned. It could have been much worse had not Dahmer stood in the blazing doorway, returning the gunfire of the attackers until the rest of the family could get out. From his hospital bed, with his lungs scorched and his face disfigured, he continued to urge Black people to get up and vote: "People who don't vote are deadbeats on the state." He died in the hospital.

When we read stories like that, we are so struck by the sheer courage that we may overlook other elements—the persistence, the ability of older activists to make common cause with younger ones, the grooming of a second generation of leadership, the willingness of rural people to defend themselves, the sense of community that allows a prosperous man to identify so deeply with his less well-off neighbors. In the Mississippi movement, as elsewhere in the rural South, these are recurrent themes.

The return of veterans from World War II and the Supreme Court's outlawing of the white primary helped stimulate Black activism across the South. In Mississippi, that activism was largely focused on the right to vote; desegregating public accommodations did not get as much attention as it did in the upper South and border states. The massive resistance triggered by the *Brown* decision included intense economic pressure aimed at activists. They were fired from their jobs and evicted from their homes. Banks refused to make the traditional crop loans, but even if they had money, stores refused to sell them supplies or buy their harvest. Doctors refused to see them; insurance companies refused to cover them. Much of this was orchestrated by the white Citizens' Council. There were also reprisals of the more traditional sort. In 1955 alone, seven civil rights leaders were slain and a much larger number driven out of state. The reprisals drove down the number of NAACP members and the number of Blacks registered to vote. The movement was not destroyed, though. By the end of the decade, local leaders were still in place and had begun to repair the damage done by the repression.

On the face of it, it would be hard to imagine a situation that offered poorer prospects for a voter registration campaign than Mississippi in 1960. All the obvious sources of power seemed to be on one side— effectively all political power, virtually all the economic resources, an incredible capacity for inflicting violence, legal and extralegal. For that reason, the older civil rights organizations were opposed to investing organizational resources in Mississippi. In fact, they underestimated the resources that Mississippi Blacks could bring to bear, including an indigenous network of activists. When younger civil rights workers came into the state, they were immediately able to build on the infrastructure that a previous generation had begun.

Because of her years supporting southern activists, Ella Baker was well acquainted with Mississippi's Black leadership. In the fall of 1960, SNCC decided to send someone to Mississippi to recruit for a conference it was organizing. Bob Moses, a New Yorker drawn south by the sit-ins, was the recruiter. Baker sent him to Amzie Moore, one of the World War II veterans who returned home determined to make Mississippi safe for democracy. Moore had been pushed to the brink of economic ruin and his life was threatened constantly, but he had built a large NAACP branch in the middle of the Mississippi Delta. A 1955 *Ebony* magazine shows a rally in the Delta, with attendance estimated at thirteen thousand. Moore is shown handing out voting instructions, and the caption notes that he started a near-riot as people fought to get the handouts.

The Mississippi movement was profoundly affected by the relationship between Moore and Moses. According to Moses, Moore's generation of leaders survived in part by becoming astute judges of character. Once Moore had decided that Moses was serious, he began to systematically teach Moses about movement history and politics in Mississippi. By late summer 1961, Moses was opening a voter registration school in McComb in the southwest corner of the state, probably the most violent section of the state. Supported by the older NAACP activists, Moses's school got off to a rapid start; he had been there only a few weeks when nearby counties started requesting schools of their own.

The response was predictable. In late August, a cousin of the sheriff accosted Moses, knocked him to the ground, and then proceeded to use the blunt end of a knife to beat him bloody. Shortly after that, they attacked another worker, Travis Britt, beating him semiconscious. Two days later, another worker, John Hardy, was pistol-whipped in the registrar's office. When it became clear that violence could not drive the SNCC people out—Moses had even taken the unprecedented step of filing charges against his attacker—the attacks turned to the local people who had supported the movement. At the end of September, one of them, Herbert Lee, was shot and killed by state legislator E. H. Hurst, who had been threatening to kill a civil rights leader.

Lee, a dairy farmer, had been an NAACP member since 1953 and a stalwart supporter of the new voter registration drive. Although the killing took place in broad daylight in front of several witnesses, Hurst never spent a day in jail. SNCC had gone into voter registration work in some of the most dangerous Deep South counties convinced they were in a partnership with Washington, that the Justice Department was going to do something to neutralize racist violence. In fact, in the face of violence against civil rights workers and local people, they learned that the government continued to make timid and minimalist responses. In some cases, including Lee's, they had reason to believe that some members of the Justice Department were even in collusion with local racists. The Justice Department could not be counted on, and the broader society showed little interest. How do you appeal to the conscience of a nation that is ignoring you?

At a terrible cost, SNCC had learned a lot in McComb. According to Moses, one of the most important lessons they learned was that they could find family in Mississippi.

> We could go anyplace in Mississippi before we were through and we knew that somewhere down some road there was family. And we could show up there unannounced with no money or no anything and there were people there ready to take care of us. . . . One of the things that happened in the movement was that there was a joining of a young generation of people with an older generation that nurtured and sustained them. . . . It was an amazing experience. . . . It's a liberating kind of experience.

Local Mississippians offered more than nurturing; they offered physical protection as well. In the rural South, the national discussion

about nonviolence was academic. Rural people who joined the movement typically saw no contradiction between self-defense and nonviolence. When nightriders shot into the home of Robert and Lillie Mae
Howard and wounded Mrs. Howard (their children had integrated the
Holmes County schools), Robert Howard retaliated with his automatic
shotgun, "but I don't figure that I was violent. All I was doin' was
protectin' myself." He spoke for hundreds of other Black farmers. Many
of the NAACP leaders who had been active in the 1950s seldom went
anyplace without being thoroughly armed. In the 1960s, communities
with high rates of Black landownership such as Mileston were especially
aggressive about setting up armed defense patrols and letting white people know the patrols were there, almost daring them to start trouble.
The movement volunteers who came into the state in 1964 were
warned that they could not go into these areas at night unless they were
expected. Outside such communities, local people who took civil rights
workers in routinely sat up at night guarding their homes against reprisals, creating a moral dilemma for the students who had argument after
argument over whether they, representing organizations that were officially nonviolent, could take their turn on guard.

White supremacist violence of the 1950s and 1960s was of a different character from that of earlier eras. Nighttime bombing and drive-by
shootings were replacing mob violence done in broad daylight. The
change was due in part to growing worry about the world outside Mississippi, including the Justice Department, but it was almost certainly
encouraged by the growing willingness of Black Mississippians to shoot
back.

In the spring of 1962, with the support of the Voter Education
Project, civil rights workers, most of them college aged, initiated registration campaigns across the state. Normally, there were only one or two
workers assigned to a county at first. Understandably, most local Blacks
initially rejected them, fearful of retribution. People who had been a
part of the activist networks of the 1950s typically gave the young workers their initial base. Others had to be won over gradually. Many people
were moved by the sheer persistence of the youngsters. A resident of
McComb said of one of them:

> Anytime a man come in my community and took the hardships that
> he took, if he was wrong, I better join with him anyway. He's ready

to take a beating, [get] jailed, being bombed and get back on two feet. . . . I'm ready to join that fellow, wherever he is, right or wrong.

A predictable pattern of response ensued. People who had a degree of economic independence from white people were often among the early joiners—independent landowners, barbers, and beauticians, for example. Teachers, on the other hand, who would have immediately been fired had they joined the movement, were especially difficult to attract. Contrary to the common impression that that movement leadership was largely ministerial, in the rural South ministers as a class were slow to find their path to the movement. Their reluctance was a frequent subject of the oratory at mass meetings. At one meeting in Greenwood in 1963, the comedian Dick Gregory, to a cheering audience, blasted preachers and teachers, saying it was:

> disgraceful that in this area, the Negro religious leaders haven't played their part. I'm a Baptist by choice, but if I had to spend much time in this area, they'd have to force me to be a Baptist because even little kids are in the struggle and not one Baptist church has opened up its doors in this area.
>
> In college, I almost decided to be a school teacher but when I see how far behind school teachers in this area are dragging their feet, I'm glad I didn't decide it. And your principal you have here. . . . When this man would ask Negro kids to stop fighting for their rights, he is lower than the lowest Negro, lower than the lowest animal that walks the face of the earth. . . . These handkerchief heads don't realize this area is going to break.

Across the South, teachers and ministers, the heart of the Black middle class in small towns, did become active later, especially after the passage of the Voting Rights Act. In the early 1960s, it was largely a movement of working-class people.

It was also a movement of women. When we think of civil rights leaders, the names that come easily to mind are mostly men. In fact, at the local level, a disproportionate share of the leadership came from women. SCLC's Andy Young has noted, "It was woman going door to door, speaking with their neighbors, meeting in voter-registration classes together, organizing through their churches that gave the vital momentum and energy to the movement, that made it a mass movement."

Across the Black Belt, it appears that women were more likely to attempt to register and attend mass meetings, citizenship classes, and the like. It is certainly not clear that women were less exposed to danger than men. Women in Mississippi were regularly clubbed at demonstrations and beaten in jail. Their homes were firebombed and shot up even when no adult males were present. We cannot be certain, but maybe the greater level of participation by women was a by-product of their religious faith. Given the objective situation in the early 1960s, the odds against the movement ever achieving anything must have seemed staggering. Faith in God made it easier to believe that the impossible could be done. The fact that SNCC was looking for untapped leadership certainly made it more likely that they would attract women.

SNCC had been profoundly influenced by Ella Baker. Its members saw themselves as organizing, not mobilizing. They took mobilizing to mean large-scale, relatively short-term public events—Birmingham, Selma, the March on Washington, the events most people associate with the movement. Organizing represents another tradition of Black activism, a tradition that places greater emphasis on the long-term development of leadership in ordinary men and women. It is a slower, often less dramatic form of activism, in which organizers are pushing other people to make their own decisions, not look to some external leadership to think for them, decide for them, fight for them. One organizer wrote friends:

> I hope this [newsletter] will give you some idea of one phase of the activity in Amite County. It is less spectacular than marches and such, but, I feel, much more meaningful. Marches help to remove some of the external barriers to the Negro people's freedom. They do little to emancipate people from within. . . . It is by talking and acting together—on their own initiative and their own decision—that some of these bonds begin to be loosed.

Thus, organizers do not want to project themselves in the way that traditional leaders do; they want to project the people with whom they are working. Organizers should be in the back of the room, not the front. Fannie Lou Hamer represented the perfect case of how SNCC organizers wanted the process to work. While most of them remained relatively anonymous outside the state, Hamer became a national media figure. Her face became the face the nation associated with the movement. For SNCC organizers, as necessary as the media were to their work at certain points in the process, the media were always problematic. Their tendency to lionize a few individuals and ignore the contributions of many others violated the egalitarian ethos of SNCC. It also had the potential of creating jealousies within the movement.

By the end of 1963, the movement and the forces of white supremacy had reached something of a stalemate. The movement had rooted itself in the lives of many local people who would no longer be stifled by violence or economic repression. On the other hand, while hundreds of people were attempting to register, few were actually being registered and lives were still being lost. The 1964 killing of Louis Allen, who had been a witness to the 1961 murder of Herbert Lee, was the last straw for many in SNCC and CORE. Something had to be done to make the federal government take a stronger stand, and the Mississippi Summer Project became that something.

It was a deal with the devil, premised on the idea that white lives matter and Black lives do not. The movement was betting that when middle-class whites lives were placed in jeopardy, Washington would stop temporizing about what it did and did not have the authority to do and find some way to protect them, which would benefit Black activists as well. They were using the racism of the nation to protect themselves from the racism of Mississippi. Most Mississippi SNCC and CORE staff were against the decision, partly out of fear that bringing in educated outsiders would undermine the work they were doing to build local leadership.

At one level, the summer was a remarkable breakthrough. It was the second-most covered news story of the year. After years of double-talk, the federal government began aggressively infiltrating and prosecuting the Klan across the Deep South. The defenders of white supremacy gradually lost their ability to use overt violence. The tactic had done what it was supposed to do. Moreover, the experience had transformed the volunteers themselves, many of whom went on to play important roles in the antiwar, feminist, and student power movements.

The cost was high. On the one hand, the summer was arguably among the most morally compelling moments in the entire history of American activism. Nearly a thousand of the sons and daughters of American privilege put their soft lives on hold and exposed themselves to unpredictable terrorism to help make possible better lives for other people. There was nothing cynical about them, nothing that smacked of political expediency. These were young people trying to bring their ideals and their country into some kind of alignment.

On the other hand, the outpouring of concern for the volunteers underscored in a visceral way the nation's ability to value only some kinds of people, and the debacle at the Democratic Convention demonstrated that even liberal leaders could not be expected to put principle above expediency. Why should any sane person want to be "integrated" into a society like that? In the eyes of some of its most energetic, socially committed young people, the society lost much of its moral capital.

The movement had initially offered the country a politics built on faith and idealism. The youngsters who attended SNCC's founding conference had a profound belief in the capacity of this country to respond to human concerns. Thus, they could talk about "nonviolence as the foundation of our purpose, the presupposition of our faith, and the manner of our action. . . . Love is the central motif of nonviolence. Love is the force by which God binds man to himself and man to man. Such love goes to the extreme; it remains loving and forgiving even in the midst of hostility." Four years later, dozens of bombings and church burnings later, after hundreds of incidents in which FBI agents watched while civil rights workers were beaten into the ground, after seeing many good and decent people lose their lives while officials sworn to defend the Constitution lied and put their own careers above the lives of the people they should have been protecting, that kind of faith in one's fellow humans seemed hopelessly naive and outdated.

When Vernon Dahmer was murdered in January 1966, the white citizens of Hattiesburg rallied around his family, raising money and offering other help. They began hiring Blacks for some "white" jobs. The president—who, in the judgment of movement people, had previously ignored the families of Blacks killed in the struggle—conveyed his deep sympathy. Four or five years previously, such gestures, had they been possible, might have mattered more. By 1966, individual acts of decency could not speak to the accumulation of bitterness in the movement. "The days of singing freedom songs and the days of combating bullets and billy clubs with love are over," wrote SNCC's Julius Lester. There would be no more begging white people to be nice. "Was this not another form of the bowing and scraping their grandparents had to do to get what they wanted?" Lester added. "Were they not acting once again as the white man wanted and expected them to? And why should they have to be brutalized, physically and spiritually, for what every other American had at birth?" They had tried speaking to the country in a language of morality and had not been heard; now they would begin a search for a language the country could not continue to ignore. The language of Malcolm X seemed to make more sense than the language of freedom songs: "Whatever I say, I'm *justified.* . . . If I say right now that we should go down and shoot fifteen Ku Klux Klansmen in the morning, you may say, well, that's insane, but you can't say that I'm not justified."

LOOKING BACK: HISTORICAL LANGUAGE AND HISTORICAL MEMORY

The movement continues to exercise a considerable hold on the American imagination. Our understanding of social change, our conceptions of leadership, our understanding of the possibilities of interracial cooperation are all affected by how we remember the movement. Even much of the language that we use to discuss social issues derives from movement days. We think of the movement as a movement for "civil rights" and against "segregation." Even those seemingly innocuous terms carry their own historical baggage.

"Segregation" became the accepted way to describe the South's racial system among both Blacks and whites. In its denotative meaning, suggesting separation between Blacks and whites, it is not a very accurate term to describe that system. The system involved plenty of integration; it just had to be on terms acceptable to white people. Indeed, the agricultural economy of the early-twentieth-century South probably afforded a good deal more interracial contact than the modern urban ghetto. "White supremacy" is a more accurate description of what the system was about. "Segregation" is the way apologists for the South liked to think of it. It implies, "We're not doing anything to Black people; we just want to keep them separate from us." It was the most innocent face one could put on that system. When we use the term as a summary term for what was going on in the South, we are unconsciously adopting the preferred euphemism of nineteenth-century white supremacist leadership.

If "segregation" is a poor way to describe the problem, "integration" may not tell us much about the solution. It is not at all clear what proportion of the Black population was interested in "integration" as a general goal. African Americans have wanted access to the privileges that white people have enjoyed and have been interested in integration as a possible avenue to those privileges, but that view is different from seeing integration as important in and of itself. Even in the 1950s, it was clear that school integration, while it would potentially put more resources into the education of Black children, also potentially meant the loss of thousands of teaching jobs for Black teachers and the destruction of schools to which Black communities often felt deeply attached, however resource-poor they were. There was also something potentially demeaning in the idea that Black children had to be sitting next to white children to learn. The first Black children to integrate the schools in a given community often found themselves in a strange position, especially if they were teenagers. While some Black people thought of them as endangering themselves for the greater good of the community, others saw them as turning their backs on that community and what it had to offer. It is probably safest to say that only a segment of the Black community had anything like an ideological commitment to "integration," while most Black people were willing to give it a try to see if it really did lead to a better life.

We might also ask how "civil rights" came to be commonly used as a summary term for the struggle of African Americans. In the late 1960s, after several civil rights bills had been passed, a certain part of white America seemed not to understand why Black Americans were still angry about their collective status. "You have your civil rights. Now what's the problem?" In part, the problem was that "civil rights" was always a narrow way to conceptualize the larger struggle. For African Americans, the struggle has always been about forging a decent place for themselves within this society, which has been understood to involve the thorny issues of economic participation and self-assertion as well as civil rights. Indeed, in the 1940s, Gunnar Myrdal had demonstrated that economic issues were the ones that Black Americans ranked first in priority. At the 1963 March on Washington—which was initially conceived as a march for jobs—SNCC's John Lewis wanted to point out that SNCC was not sure it could support what became the Civil Rights Act of 1964 partly because it did not have an economic component:

> What is in the bill that will protect the homeless and starving people
> of this nation? What is there in this bill to insure the equality of a maid
> who earns $5.00 a week in the home of a family whose income is
> $100,000 a year?

One hypothesis, of course, would be that "civil rights" becomes so popular precisely because it is so narrow, precisely because it does not suggest that distribution of privilege is a part of the problem.

The "civil rights" language also implies the movement was about
Negroes; they were the ones who did not have "civil rights." From the
viewpoint of a Septima Clark or an Ella Baker, the movement was about
enriching American democracy, and those in whose name it was made
were not the only ones who profited from it. The movement helped
Chicanos, Native Americans, women, and others demand more voice
in the decisions and definitions that affected their lives. It is not immediately clear who benefited most from the movement, Black southerners
or white ones. Would the post-1960s expansion of southern economies
have been possible without the prior destruction of the South's archaic
political and economic structures? The movement made it possible for
the South to join the twentieth century.

What kind of language should we use to summarize what was
achieved by the movement of the 1960s? Activists of the period often
referred to it as a "revolution," and contemporary scholars often accept
that usage or refer to it as having "transformed" race relations in the
South. There may be an element of premature self-congratulation in this
language as well. There is something strange about taking privileges that
other people have taken for granted from the moment they came to
these shores and acting as if there is some kind of sublime moral victory
when they are finally "given" to Black people. "Oh, joy, we let the
niggers vote. Ain't we grand?" If we were talking about some group
other than Blacks being admitted to the basic rights of citizenship, one
suspects a less giddy rhetoric might be employed. Malcolm X used to
say that a man can stick a knife a foot deep into your back, wiggle it out
six inches and start yelling about how much progress we're making.
Even if he did pull the knife all the way out, Malcolm concluded, it was
going to leave a wound.

A case can be made that much of the language we use actually
obscures the nature and complexity of the movement. Similarly, a case

can be made that the way in which Martin Luther King is remembered—or disremembered, if you will—contributes to a dumbing down of the discussion. The King of popular memory is the King of August 1963, calling the peaceful throng to the ideal of brotherhood. That memory hardly does justice to the mature King. In the final years of his life, he articulated a more challenging vision of the American future and a more pessimistic assessment of America's capacity for achieving it. Thus, in those years, he was constantly at odds with the press, the White House, and much of the liberal establishment.

There was no way he could have avoided getting caught up in the Black power turmoil. The term derived much of its impact from the fact that it made white people uneasy, to understate the matter. King went to great lengths to explain it in less threatening ways, but he also refused to disavow the young people, many of whom he had worked with for years, who kept shoving the term in the nation's face. Other leaders of older civil rights organizations felt they had to distance themselves from the new radicalism, at least in part because they were worried about the loss of white support. King refused to join the general condemnation. He came to feel that some whites were exploiting the Black power controversy, using it as an excuse not to think about correcting social injustice. This was a part of King's growing disenchantment with liberal America. Too many who styled themselves liberal were only concerned with the problem when they could think of it as a southern problem, not as something in their own backyards. Too many could react supportively when racist violence was being directed against Negroes but were not much concerned with racial inequality as an evil in and of itself, could not see that poverty itself was violence, that the ghetto represented institutionalized violence against its inhabitants.

In his last years, King showed considerable capacity for sticking with what he saw as the principled position even when it was clearly costing him support. He was publically opposed to the Vietnam War when most of the country still supported it. With few exceptions, his advisers encouraged him to downplay his opposition. King did just the opposite; his criticism grew more caustic. On April 4, 1967, a year before his death, he gave a speech at Riverside Church in New York that did not equivocate.

> We must stop now. I speak as a child of God and brother to the
> suffering poor of Vietnam. I speak for those whose land is being laid
> waste, whose homes are being destroyed, whose culture is being sub-
> verted. I speak for the poor of America who are paying the double
> price of smashed hopes at home and death and corruption in Vietnam.
> I speak as a citizen of the world. . . . The great initiative in this war
> has been ours. The initiative to stop it must be ours.

The national press spent the next week castigating him. The *New York
Times* warned that "to divert the energies of the civil rights movement
to the Vietnam issue is both wasteful and self-defeating." The *Washington Post* concluded that he "has diminished his usefulness to his cause, to
his country and to his people." The *Chicago Tribune* warned Negroes
that if they wanted to continue to make progress, "they had better get
responsible leadership and repudiate the Kings and the Carmichaels."
These remarks pretty well reflect the tone of national press coverage of
King in his last year.

His criticism of the Vietnam adventure caused a further deteriora-
tion of his relationship with the White House. His relationship with the
FBI was already about as bad as it could get. The bureau—which had
labeled the "I Have a Dream" speech "demagogic"—had long been
engaged in a campaign to destroy King, taking every opportunity to feed
rumors and negative information about him to opinion leaders here and
abroad, even trying at one point to trick him into committing suicide.
J. Edgar Hoover publically called King "the most notorious liar in
America" and privately called him "the burrhead."

King's growing radicalism meant increasing skepticism about
whether the nation's conscience could be reached on economic matters,
that he put increasing emphasis on racism as a national problem, not a
regional one, and as a problem closely tied to economic exploitation. It
meant that he increasingly described problems of inequality in structural
terms, not in terms of individual prejudice.

> If we look honestly at the realities of our national life, it is clear that
> we are not marching forward: we are groping and stumbling; we are
> divided and confused. Our moral values and our spiritual confidence
> sink, even as our material wealth ascends. In these trying circum-
> stances, the black revolution is much more than a struggle for the
> rights of Negroes. It is forcing America to face all its interrelated flaws

of racism, poverty, militarism and materialism. It is exposing evils that are deeply rooted in the whole structure of our society. It reveals systemic rather than superficial flaws and suggests that radical reconstruction of society itself is the real issue to be faced.

In public discourse, he avoided the term *socialism* because it engendered such an emotional response, but at the end of his life, his vision of the good society included some form of democratic socialism.

Popular images of King tend to remember his emphasis on brotherhood and interracialism while conveniently forgetting that he saw them in the context of a structural transformation of society. The "I Have a Dream" speech remains so popular, we might suspect, because it does not suggest that social change is going to cost anybody anything. "In death," Adam Fairclough wrote:

> King became a symbol of national unity, a moderate reformer from the South, a foe of irresponsible militants, a deeply "American" figure whose achievements testified to the resilience of American democratic ideals. The uncompromising opponent of the Vietnam War, the harsh judge of American racism, the scathing critic of free enterprise, the militant advocate of "poor people's power" had to be quickly forgotten.

Ironically, King's memory is typically constructed in a way that makes it less likely that Americans will have the discussion to which he was inviting them. His memory obscures the message of his life.

We might say much the same about how the memory of Malcolm X has been constructed. There was a good deal more to him than the prophet of rage. Indeed, if one looks at the last years of these men's lives, the gap between King's thinking and Malcolm's is less than one might expect. If King was an advocate of fundamental economic restructuring, so was Malcolm X, and he was not reluctant to talk about it bluntly: "You show me a capitalist and I'll show you a bloodsucker."

King's nonviolence is often juxtaposed to Malcolm's presumed support for violence, but that does not do Malcolm's position justice. Malcolm put different spins on it at different times—including times when he seemed deliberately provocative—but the central point for him seemed to be that Blacks should pursue their liberation "by any means necessary." This view meant that violence was an option, but that is different from saying it was his program. "I don't advocate violence," he said in a 1965 speech. "But if a man steps on my toes, I'll step on his." It may be even closer to the truth to say that Malcolm's violence was largely symbolic. Maintaining that Blacks have the right to self-defense is another way of affirming their membership in a common humanity. Expecting them always to respond to humiliation and injury with meekness and love is to expect the superhuman.

As a Muslim, Malcolm X enthusiastically preached the party line about white devils, but after he left them, he denied that there were fundamental differences among people based on race. "I believe, as the Koran teaches, that a man should not be judged by the color of his skin but rather by his conscious behavior, by his actions, by his attitude toward others and his actions towards others. . . . I believe in recognizing every human being as a human being, neither white, black, brown nor red." King could not have said it better.

On one issue, King and Malcolm thought pretty much alike from the beginning. When it came to gender, both held rigid, traditional views. Ella Baker thought that King had difficulty relating to women as equals, and the only two women who served on the SCLC board during his tenure felt essentially the same way. During his Nation of Islam period, Malcolm's attitudes toward women were remarkably backward, referring to them as "deceitful, untrustworthy flesh" and the like. Nonetheless, we have more evidence that Malcolm was changing in this respect than we have for King. Late in his life, Malcolm claimed that he had learned from his travels to the Middle East and Africa that societies could not be liberated if women were not. Over the objections of some of his more traditional comrades, he insisted that women were going to hold positions of real power in his Organization of African American Unity. He told one colleague that one of the things he most regretted in his life was having taught the brothers to "spit fire" at the sisters. It is popular to play "What if?" games about what might have happened had Malcolm lived longer. Malcolm was almost certainly the most influential nationalist figure of his day. Had he lived, could his voice have helped counter some of the sexist tendencies in the nationalist organizations that proliferated in the late 1960s?

In the tumultuous final months of his life, Malcolm was reexamining old assumptions ("I'm not dogmatic about anything. I don't intend to get into any more straitjackets."). We cannot know where he would have come down, but it seems clear that without giving up his uncompromising nationalism, he was inviting us to a discussion much more complex than "violence versus nonviolence." There is a complexity and depth in his thinking that gets lost when he is reduced to the one-dimensional, fist-shaking man at the podium.

The way we "remember" King and Malcolm X is, of course, only illustrative of the way we remember the larger movement. We tend to construct our memories in ways that make us feel good but that also obscure much of what the movement was trying to say. In 1998, for example, David Halberstram, who covered the movement as a journalist, wrote an admiring essay about the courage and the impact of the early sit-in participants:

> Consider what they did. When they had started out, they were virtually alone. Only the Supreme Court . . . seemed sympathetic. . . . Yet only five years later both parties in the Congress were competing to pass legislation trying to outlaw voting injustices; the Justice Department had become their activist partner; the FBI, however reluctantly, had come aboard; and the President of the United States, Lyndon Johnson, was their principal convert. . . . What they had accomplished in that brief time span still strikes me as a shining example of democracy at work.

There are arguable interpretations here, to be mild about it, but that's not the most important issue. The problem is that the thinking here is a perspective, just one possible perspective on the movement but one that few Americans are likely to recognize as such. From another perspective, we could emphasize another set of "facts" in summation of the movement—the many innocent lives, lives of some of the least privileged of Americans, that had to be sacrificed to make the Justice Department "activist"; the way federal agencies "came aboard" partly to control the movement; the way in which Black radicalism made civil rights legislation seem like a cheap way out; the fact that many of the young people who gave the movement so much of its dynamism think that what they experienced was not some shining example of democracy but the betrayal of it. The more one appreciates the price a small number of people paid to liberate us from our past, the less miraculous the whole thing seems. Depending on how it is framed, even stressing the courage and idealism of the young people can be a dangerous game. The youngsters developed a series of powerful questions about how this society generates and sustains inequality. We praise their courage while ignoring their questions. In that context, "Our civil rights activists sure were brave" may serve the same ideological function for this generation that "Our nigras are happy" served for another, a way of denying the need for discussion of underlying problems.

Both the movement's achievements and its shortcomings can be taken out of context. If some seem prone to romanticizing the accomplishments of the movement, others, including some Black youth, seem to think the movement accomplished little or nothing, that racism is unchanged from what it used to be. In part, this thinking may reflect how little contemporary youngsters understand just what racism used to be. In part, it may be that some of them are proceeding from a Hollywoodesque version of historical change, where all problems have to be resolved by the last scene. Thinking about history in that way stands in sharp contrast to the way many movement veterans thought about it. They understood their lives as chapters in an ongoing struggle. Ella Baker, who had organized Black history programs in the 1920s and was organizing against South African apartheid in the 1970s, was asked once how she had kept at it so long. She answered in terms that reflected one enduring vision of the movement:

> But if people begin to place their values in terms of how high they get in the political world, or how much worldly goods they accumulate, or what kind of cars they have, or how much they have in the bank, that's where I begin to lose respect. To me, I'm part of the human family. What the human family will accomplish, I can't control. But it isn't impossible that what those who came along with me went through, might stimulate others to continue to fight for a society that does not have those kinds of problems. Somewhere down the line the numbers increase, the tribe increases. So how do you keep on? I can't help it. I don't claim to have any corner on an answer, but I believe the struggle is eternal. Somebody else carries on.

POSTSCRIPT: THE LEGACY OF MARTIN LUTHER KING, JR.

Which of the following best reflects your understanding of the role of Martin Luther King, Jr. in the civil rights movement?

A. Dr. King was the main force behind the civil rights movement, its chief strategist and most important leader.

B. The course of the movement was influenced by a great many people, among whom Dr. King was perhaps the most visible and best known to those outside the movement.

Mind you, assessing the impact of any individual on a complicated social movement is an inherently difficult task, all the more so in cases in which participants themselves have widely divergent opinions, which is the case here. Beware of confusing notoriety with impact. Consider, too, that your response will say as much about you as about your historical knowledge. The way you respond to the question is likely to reflect your own attitudes, hopes, and fears about the American racial situation, your assumptions about which changes matter, as well as your assumptions about what the movement was trying to do.

It is not clear that anyone really regards King "as merely one among many leaders" but many, especially among those who committed a substantial part of their life to the movement, question the idea that King was somehow the central force behind the movement. Thus, this questioning is not merely the viewpoint of young militants born after the movement. In 1965, August Meier, one of the deans of civil rights historiography, wrote an assessment of "the phenomenon that is Martin Luther King," noting the paradox that while much of the outside world saw him as *the* civil rights leader, many within the movement criticized him for what they saw as his conservatism, his indecisiveness, his tendency to premature compromise, his unwillingness to expose himself to the physical risks that other activists had to face, his investment in currying favor with the powerful, as well as for being isolated and aloof. For most of the period between the Montgomery bus boycott and the 1963 Birmingham campaign, "King appeared not to direct but to float with the tide of militant direct action."

King's real importance, Meier contends, inhered in his ability to articulate Black demands in ways which resonated deeply for many audiences, Black and white. In particular, his "conservative militance," as Meier terms it, gave white people to understand that they had to change but that "he is their good friend, that he poses no threat to them." Thus, King played a particularly important role in making the movement respectable. In this, he was aided by the existence of more frightening alternatives. "King would be neither respected nor respectable if there were not more militant activists on his left, engaged in more radical forms of direct action." At the same time, precisely because he was a centrist, in both temperament and politics, King was able to keep channels of communication open, not only between activists and much of the nonactivist white community, but between different wings of the movement as well. Under this interpretation, King played a role that few others would have been equipped to play, but that is far different from saying that he was the central force behind the movement. With due allowance for variations in emphasis, that kind of more nuanced assessment of King would have represented the view of many scholars, activists, and intellectuals whose understanding of the movement wasn't filtered through the popular press.

In 1963, the leaders of the Birmingham movement decided that the honor of announcing that a desegregation agreement had been reached should go to Fred Shuttlesworth, in recognition of his long and valiant struggle, without which the Birmingham movement of 1963 would probably not have been possible. As one biographer of King put it, "Although Shuttlesworth announced the terms of the settlement, the reporters would not be satisfied until they heard it from King himself, as most of their readers knew nothing about Shuttlesworth." Most of the nation saw the movement through the eyes of a national press corps that understood little about either the roots of local struggles or the internal dynamics of Black communities. It would be an oversimplification to say that the media made King; poll data, among other sources, indicates that many ordinary Black Americans felt a profound connection to him. Nevertheless, King became an important part of the media framing of the civil rights story, which meant that his name and voice became associated with initiatives neither he nor SCLC had started or in which they played a marginal role: the sit-ins; the freedom rides; Birmingham; the Albany, Georgia campaign; the Selma campaign. As noted earlier, in some of these cases, including Albany and Selma, King's involvement brought new levels of attention and energy, but it did so at the cost of obscuring the role of others who made the initiatives possible. The press tended to see only the final act and reported that as if it were the whole story.

Insisting that the movement was larger than Dr. King does him no dishonor. The reassessment of King in recent decades is less a rewriting of history than a correction of it, bringing popular understandings of his role more closely into alignment with the views of many of those who were closest to the movement. We can be sure that treatments of the movement, which virtually reduce it to Dr. King, mask the wide diversity of opinions and political styles among African Americans and do violence to our collective understanding of how deliberate social change gets made. Perhaps the most important point to remember about King is not that he "led" the movement but that the movement gave him a platform from which he could appeal to the long-slumbering angels of our better nature, which he did as well as any leader of his time, probably better. That is honor enough.

Documents

1

EXCERPT FROM ELLA J. BAKER'S "BIGGER THAN A HAMBURGER" (JUNE 1960)

[Editor's note: Baker's comments on the Raleigh, North Carolina, meeting out of which SNCC grew (a meeting that she called) capture the core of her political philosophy.]

RALEIGH, N.C.—The Student Leadership Conference made it crystal clear that current sit-ins and other demonstrations are concerned with something much bigger than a hamburger or even a giant-sized Coke.

Whatever may be the difference in approach to their goal, the Negro and white students, North and South, are seeking to rid America of the scourge of racial segregation and discrimination—not only at lunch counters, but in every aspect of life.

In reports, casual conversations, discussion groups, and speeches, the sense of the spirit of the following statement that appeared in the initial newsletter of the students at Barber-Scotia College, Concord, N.C., were re-echoed time and again:

> We want the world to know that we no longer accept the inferior position of second-class citizenship. We are willing to go to jail, be ridiculed, spat upon and even suffer physical violence to obtain First Class Citizenship.

By and large, this feeling that they have a destined date with freedom, was not limited to a drive for personal freedom, or even freedom for the Negro in the South. Repeatedly it was emphasized that the movement

159

was concerned with the moral implications of racial discrimination for the "whole world" and the "Human Race."

This universality of approach was linked with a perceptive recognition that "it is important to keep the movement democratic and to avoid struggles for personal leadership."

It was further evident that desire for supportive cooperation from adult leaders and the adult community was also tempered by apprehension that adults might try to "capture" the student movement. The students showed willingness to be met on the basis of equality, but were intolerant of anything that smacked of manipulation or domination.

This inclination toward *group-centered leadership,* rather than toward a *leader-centered group pattern of organization,* was refreshing indeed to those of the older group who bear the scars of the battle, the frustrations and the disillusionment that come when the prophetic leader turns out to have heavy feet of clay.

However hopeful might be the signs in the direction of group-centeredness, the fact that many schools and communities, especially in the South, have not provided adequate experience for young Negroes to assume initiative and think and act independently accentuated the need for guarding the student movement against well-meaning, but nevertheless unhealthy, overprotectiveness.

Here is an opportunity for adults and youth to work together and provide genuine leadership—the development of the individual to his highest potential for the benefit of the group.

Many adults and youth characterized the Raleigh meeting as the greatest or most significant conference of our period.

Whether it lives up to this high evaluation or not will, in a large measure, be determined by the extent to which there is more effective training in and understanding of non-violent principles and practices, in group dynamics, and in the re-direction into creative channels of the normal frustrations and hostilities that result from second-class citizenship. . . .

2

HANDBILL, ALBANY NONVIOLENT MOVEMENT (NOVEMBER 9, 1961)

THE ALBANY NONVIOLENT MOVEMENT
MEETS
THURSDAY 7 pm NOVEMBER 9th
MACEDONIA BAPTIST CHURCH
CORNER JEFFERSON & CHERRY
REV. L.W. WHITE

To those who love the Lord and Freedom:

COME; LISTEN; LEARN; LOVE!

"We believe in the Fatherhood of God and the brotherhood of man. We believe that God made of one blood all nations for to dwell on all the face of the earth."

Our beliefs have consequences.
If we are of one blood, children of one common Father, brothers in the household of God, then we must be of equal worth in His family, entitled to equal opportunity in the society of men. That "all men are created equal, that they are endowed by their creator with certain unalienable rights, that among these are life, liberty and the pursuit of happiness," we hold to be self evident.
Moreover, if there is the seed of God in every man, then every man

161

has, by reason of that fact alone, worth and dignity. It follows that no man may, with impunity, discriminate against or exploit another. And if the nature of man is such as we affirmed, then nothing less than its full recognition, nothing less than the dignity and respect due him simply because he is a man, can ever satisfy him.

Our faith leads us one step further. Like responds to like for the most part. If there is in every man a measure of goodness and truth, this quality will respond when it meets its kind and truth and goodness have no color. We are called upon, therefore, to love our fellow men, all of them, with all the risks that that implies and all the privileges that it promises.

Our faith is incurably optimistic and unyieldingly realistic. It teaches us that we live in an ordered universe in which the moral law of cause and effect, of means and ends, is as unchangeable as any physical law. *Violence corrupts* and destroys both the user and the victim; *the power of Love and Nonviolence is creative and redeems both.*

In such a faith we look forward with confidence to a new day when man will be measured by what he is and not by his race, creed, color, or nationality. That day can be near if we go forward with energy, faith, and knowledge. It can be very far away if we respond with fear and ignorance. In that day each man will be free to contribute to his fullest capacity for the good of all men; his opportunity to develop will not be curtailed. Segregation and second-class citizenship will take their places with slavery as evils of the past. No two men will be alike; but no two will be different in value to society because of race, color, religion, or nationality. Just as we now know that all are hurt by injury to any one, so in that tomorrow all will benefit by the achievement of each. As prejudice feeds on prejudice, so brotherhood will feed on brotherhood.

SUPPORT THE STUDENTS
COME
MACEDONIA BAPTIST CHURCH
"We Shall Overcome"

3

CHRONOLOGY OF VIOLENCE AND INTIMIDATION IN MISSISSIPPI 1961 (1963)

. . . AUGUST 15, AMITE COUNTY: Robert Moses, Student Nonviolent Coordinating Committee (SNCC) registration worker, and three Negroes who had tried unsuccessfully to register in Liberty, were driving toward McComb when a county officer stopped them. He asked if Moses was the man ". . . who's been trying to register our niggers." All were taken to court and Moses was arrested for "impeding an officer in the discharge of his duties," fined $50 and spent two days in jail.

AUGUST 22, AMITE COUNTY: Robert Moses went to Liberty with three Negroes, who made an unsuccessful attempt to register. A block from the courthouse, Moses was attacked and beaten by Billy Jack Caston, the sheriff's first cousin. Eight stitches were required to close a wound in Moses' head. Caston was acquitted of assault charges by an all-white jury before a justice of the peace.

AUGUST 26, MC COMB, PIKE COUNTY: Hollis Watkins, 20, and Elmer Hayes, 20, SNCC workers, were arrested while staging a sit-in at the F. W. Woolworth store and charged with breach of the peace. They spent 36 days in jail.

AUGUST 27 AND 29, MC COMB, PIKE COUNTY: Five Negro students from a local high school were convicted of breach of the peace following a sit-in at a variety store and bus terminal. They were sentenced to a $400 fine each and eight months in jail. One of these students, a girl of 15, was turned over to juvenile authorities, released, subsequently rearrested, and sentenced to 12 months in a state school for delinquents.

AUGUST 29, MC COMB, PIKE COUNTY: Two Negro leaders were arrested in McComb as an aftermath of the sit-in protest march on city hall, charged with contributing to the delinquency of minors. They were Curtis C. Bryant of McComb, an official of the NAACP, and Cordelle Reagan, of SNCC. Each arrest was made on an affidavit signed by Police Chief George Guy, who said he had information that the two ". . . were behind some of this racial trouble."

AUGUST 30, MC COMB, PIKE COUNTY: SNCC workers Brenda Travis, 16, Robert Talbert, 19, and Isaac Lewis, 20, staged a sit-in in the McComb terminal of the Greyhound bus lines. They were arrested on charges of breach of the peace and failure to obey a policeman's order to move on. They spent 30 days in jail.

SEPTEMBER 5, LIBERTY, AMITE COUNTY: Travis Britt, SNCC registration worker, was attacked and beaten by whites on the courthouse lawn. Britt was accompanied at the time by Robert Moses. Britt said one man hit him more than 20 times. The attackers drove away in a truck.

SEPTEMBER 7, TYLERTOWN, WALTHALL COUNTY: John Hardy, SNCC registration worker, took two Negroes to the county courthouse to register. The registrar told them he ". . . wasn't registering voters" that day. When the three turned to leave, Registrar John Q. Wood took a pistol from his desk and struck Hardy over the head from behind. Hardy was arrested and charged with disturbing the peace.

SEPTEMBER 13, JACKSON, HINDS COUNTY: Fifteen Episcopal ministers (among them three Negroes) were arrested for asking to be served at the lunch counter of the Greyhound bus terminal. They were charged with inviting a breach of the peace. They were found not guilty of the charge on May 21, 1962, by County Judge Russell Moore.

SEPTEMBER 25, LIBERTY, AMITE COUNTY: Herbert Lee, a Negro who had been active in voter registration, was shot and killed by white state representative E. H. Hurst in downtown Liberty. No prosecution was undertaken, the authorities explaining that the representative had shot in self-defense.

OCTOBER 4, MC COMB, PIKE COUNTY: The five students who were arrested as a result of the August 29 sit-in in McComb returned to school, but were refused admittance. At that, 116 students walked out and paraded downtown to the city hall in protest. Police arrested the entire crowd, but later released all but 19, all of whom were 18 years old or older. They were charged with breach of the peace and contributing to the delinquency of minors and allowed to go free on bail totalling $3,700. At the trial on October 31, Judge Brumfield, finding the students guilty, and sentencing each to a $500 fine and six months in jail, said: "Some of you are local residents, some of you are outsiders. Those of you who are local residents are like sheep being led to the slaughter. If you continue to follow the advise of outside agitators, you will be like sheep and be slaughtered."

4

STUDENT VOICE EDITORIAL AND CARTOON ON THE FBI (NOVEMBER 25, 1964)

[Editor's note: The editorial and cartoon reflect the movement's disgust with the FBI in particular, part of a growing disenchantment with the federal government, a disenchantment that undermined nonviolent optimism.]

The Director of the Federal Bureau of Investigation, J. Edgar Hoover, could spend his time more wisely finding the midnight bombers, arsonists and murderers throughout the South and directing his agents to use their powers under Federal law to make on the spot arrests of Southern policemen who daily deny Negroes their constitutional rights, than in trying to justify the historic failure of the FBI to make any concrete advances in assuring that Southern Negroes can exercise the simplest rights that most Americans take for granted.

The FBI, especially under Hoover, is incapable of performing this task. Such a task would require arresting many of the law enforcement officials with whom the FBI works with and cooperates with daily in the course of their investigations.

For Negroes the FBI has become part of the oppression of the South.

The FBI under Hoover has come to mean, "the man" and the police state to Southern Negroes.

The FBI under Hoover has come to mean an organization that stands and watches as Negroes are beaten in Selma, Ala. because it is an "investigatory agency."

The FBI under Hoover has come to mean an organization that can't find the killers of Louis Allen and Goodman, Schwerner and Chaney.

The FBI under Hoover has come to stand for an organization that can not protect any person, in his attempt to register to vote.

The FBI under Hoover has come to stand for an organization that disregards Federal laws for the sake of local officials. We have repeatedly emphasized that the FBI has the power to act and to make arrests without warrants for "any offense against the United States committed in their presence;" and arrest anybody they believe has committed a felony if they have reasonable grounds to believe that the person has committed such a felony.

It is now time to end the Hoover version of the FBI.

SCENES OF THE SOUTH BY WEAVER

5

POSTER FROM EAST SELMA, ALABAMA, FROM THE *STUDENT VOICE* (AUGUST 30, 1965)

[Editor's note: A backyard barbecue may be "less spectacular than marches and such," but from an organizer's viewpoint it can be part of the process by which people get pulled into the movement.]

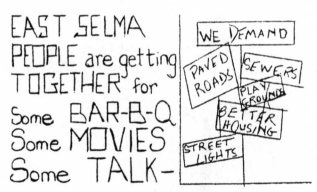

EAST SELMA PEOPLE are getting TOGETHER for Some BAR-B-Q Some MOVIES Some TALK—

WE DEMAND PAVED ROADS SEWERS PLAY GROUND BETTER HOUSING STREET LIGHTS

Some talk about Some of the Things
That Need to be Done
In East Selma
Some talk about How to get These
Things Done

COME and BRING YOUR NEIGHBORS
to The East Selma People's Convention

at CLAUDIA MAE STRONG'S BACKYARD
220 HALL ST. (NEAR MAXEY)

EAST SELMA, ALABAMA—Residents of Selma's all Negro East side gathered together in mid-July to discuss improving city services in their neighborhood.

Meetings like this one are planned for other Alabama communities, and hopefully will begin building a base of interest in community affairs.

6

"THIS TRANSFORMATION OF PEOPLE": AN INTERVIEW WITH BOB MOSES

From 1961 to 1965, Bob Moses was a field secretary for the Student Nonviolent Coordinating Committee in Mississippi, a key figure in the struggle to obtain the right to vote for African Americans in that state and one of the movement's staunchest advocates for grassroots organizing centered on developing the capacity of local leadership. Currently, he is the national director of the Algebra Project, an attempt to use the lessons and the spirit of the sixties movement to attack some of the barriers constricting the lives of inner-city youngsters and rural poor youngsters. In this interview, conducted in August 1993, he elaborates on the many-layered concept of organizing, on the contemporary relevance of the sixties movement, on the processes that develop and sustain activist personalities, and on some of the people who most influenced him.

> I want to tell you about Mrs. Hazel Palmer, who is a lady who works with the Freedom Democratic Party in Mississippi. She was working for ten, fifteen dollars a week as a maid most of her life. She stopped and changed last summer. And if you want to write her, and I suggest you do—a lot of you—drop her a line. Ask her, "What did you use to do? What do you do now? How come you changed? What gave you the courage to do that? What makes you think that instead of being a cook in somebody's kitchen you could help run a political party? Where did you go to learn how to do that? Did you go to school?
>
> Bob Moses, 1965

PAYNE: When you think about empowering leadership at the grassroots level, do particular examples come to mind?

170

MOSES: Well, Mrs. Palmer.

PAYNE: Hazel Palmer?

MOSES: Yeah. . . . She really came to symbolize for me this sort of empowerment of the grassroots people, this leadership phenomenon that Ella [Baker] pointed us to and she never became a media person. She always worked behind the scenes in the Freedom Democratic Party. She had been the janitor at one of the local schools and then her children got involved in the freedom rides in '61 and then she began to work with Medgar [Evers] and then when Medgar was assassinated in '63, she came over to the COFO [Council of Federated Organizations, the alliance of civil rights organizations in Mississippi] office and started working with us. And then she got involved in the Freedom Democratic Party and became sort of the chief networking person out of the Jackson office on the Watts line, so she really would do a whole lot of the calling and networking with groups across the country and really became very sophisticated in her understanding of the movement and the organizing, what the movement was trying to do with poor people like her. The last time I met with her before she died, they had these people over at Duke [University] who had this program where they would bring in people. It was a sort of community leadership kind of program, so they brought people in to talk. They asked me to come in and I said I would if they would bring Mrs. Palmer, too. So, they did and the two of us did an all-day workshop and it was, it was really moving to watch her speak with the students. Her life had gone full-circle since the movement days. She was back in Jackson, running a washeteria, which was sort of right next to where she lived. It was just an old, run-down washeteria. People would come in to do their clothes. She didn't have the sort of credentials, any of the academic credentials or otherwise credentials, to move into any kind of professional world or move into the politics that emerged in Mississippi the way they emerged and in Jackson, the Jackson politics, I think, got taken over by the Black middle class. [It might have been different] maybe, if she lived in Holmes County where they still had their own, growing MFDP [Mississippi Freedom Democratic Party] network. So, [after the movement], she went back into what she had been doing before except that the movement had left its mark on her. So, here we had this woman who was living, you know, this very bottomed-out life, doing the washeteria and so forth, living and struggling with kids who were growing up and not doing all that well. But, who could go to Duke and really talk to these white, middle-class kids and touch them in a way that very few people could just because of what she had absorbed over the years, through the movement in combination with the life that she had lived.

So, Mrs. Palmer, I used to go around and talk about her because she really came to represent what we were looking at trying to do in the community organizing because there was, I think there's a dimension to it, which is dealing with this transformation of people. Outside of the institutions, which are normally credentializing people and sort of giving the kind of support which allows them to feel, "Well, I can really play this role," Mrs. Hamer always used to say, that she got that kind of support from the SNCC people, that, you know, you just keep telling them what you're telling them. Just keep saying what you're saying, right. That kind of support sort of plays the role of institutional support. Someone who comes out of either a major educational institution or a labor union movement kind of thing, or certain kind of church institutions gets credentialized and part of what the institution does is make them feel like they have the ability and the right and the know-how to play certain roles. And, I think part of what the organizing thrust in the movement and what Ella was talking about in terms of leadership is that kind of credentializing. That if you have a movement, then part of what is a sign that you do have such a movement is that people begin to emerge, to feel power and act in power and to actually play a very different role than they may have been playing and they do this because of the context of the movement; they haven't been otherwise credentialized, going off to school, going off to some other institution to do this stuff. It's the force of the movement, the feel that the movement creates. I think in Mississippi, you saw a number of women emerge who did that. So, Mrs. Palmer was one. Mrs. Hamer, who became well known, was one. Annie Devine was another. Mrs. [Victoria] Gray, out of Hattiesburg was another. Mrs. [Winnie] Hudson. . . . Because it seems to me that Mississippi was really unique in turning up this group of women who played this major role in shaping that state. I don't think there's quite another experience like that. When you have people who, really all of them were not coming out of any sort of educational background having been credentialized. . . . So, this, it's an element about the organizing which is hard to sort of pin down. 'Cause you think about organizing, people think more about the networking and the building of some kind of structures, working some kind of programs, setting out some particular goals that you're going to accomplish as opposed to this setting up something which becomes a kind of field or force, some kind of culture through which people can actually emerge and do in fact emerge. That is, that it actually happens.

PAYNE: What is there about that culture in Mississippi that attracted so many women or is it something that can be pinpointed?

MOSES: I am not sure. Part of it, of course, was that within the NAACP, the leadership was really male-dominated. Now, clearly one thing the movement did in Mississippi was open up space for women to emerge because they did emerge. So, clearly the movement provided some space for that to happen. I am not sure why. I don't remember that there was any conscious thinking, you know. We weren't thinking that way, but . . . I think, there was somehow just the recognition in looking for whoever. . . .

PAYNE: . . . was willing to step forward.

MOSES: That's right. Going to step forward. Now, why women stepped forward, I don't know.

PAYNE: I want to go back to what you were saying about the transformative experiences. With the Algebra Project, which I guess is close to ten years old now, has that changed your sense about how people go through that? About how you structure an environment and a culture that makes that transformation more likely?

MOSES: Well, you're watching it, some people within the Project are watching it with some teachers, right. So, you're seeing it happening through the workshops and the classroom experience. And this larger framework, right, it's not something that can happen if the framework is narrow. I think they've got to be exposed to a lot. Part of what the movement did was just expose people to a lot. I mean it was exposing people to all different kinds of people who were coming in and out of Mississippi. Exposing people to people by taking them out of Mississippi, traveling and meeting people elsewhere. And the people that they're meeting are all people who are somehow part of this movement culture. They share in certain values and [are] talking about certain things. So, that is also part of what I think is happening or has to happen for people to begin to do that here [with the Algebra Project]. A teacher is seeing something different in how she relates to people in her classroom and in her school, but then she's also relating to a wider nexus of people in some other activity. It may be a training activity, but then she's also relating to a wider network at large meetings. They're going to these national meetings and then meeting people from all different walks of life and different parts of the country. If all of those activities are really sort of trying to get across the same message, which is that people have to take ownership over what they're doing. They have to commit themselves and there has to be this element of persistence and also an element of looking, trying to figure out how to work with other people. If all of that is happening everywhere, then it begins to be more than just the sum of the parts. Something begins to take hold, which becomes sort of a culture, which then provides a place where people can grow and emerge. So, you're watching it. You see it happening. You see a little of it happening [in the Algebra Project]. . . . We don't know how to start a movement. I mean, no one knows how to do that. People who've been in the movement can recognize it when they see it. . . . [We spoke about the training provided by Septima Clark's Citizenship Schools.] . . . Our network was identifying people who were good candidates to go to that training. And, then that training, is part of this process which is going on where people are now meeting other people and exchanging all of these values and really becoming part of some larger movement. So, it becomes something that's helpful, really supporting. Part of what allowed that to happen is just saying, "Well, even though these organizations aren't talking to each other at the top, in Mississippi, this is all one thing."

PAYNE: It's all the same people at the bottom.

MOSES: Right. It's all the same people. So this COFO set-up allows you now to take advantage of really what was the best parts of the movement culture. So you could send people over there and this became part of this movement culture, which they're experiencing, which isn't any organization's culture. It doesn't belong to one organization. It's something, almost by definition, if you've got it, you've got a number of organizations which are somehow intertwined there. Because it means that there's some central issue or idea which has grabbed enough people that people who otherwise wouldn't be working on the same thing are now all working on the same thing, from different points of view.

PAYNE: And individual organizational identity becomes less important than whatever that larger issue is?

MOSES: For some people. But, it's that for all your grassroots people who really don't think of themselves as being this organizational person or that organizational person. But, they think of themselves as really caught up in whatever this problem is and needing to work with whomever. It was Webb Owens in McComb who really drove this home to me. I mean he said it a thousand times if he said it once during those first six months in '61 when I got down there, which was, "I belong to the NAACP. I belong to CORE. I belong with SNCC. I belong to *anything* which is going to help this Black man in Mississippi." He just kept drumming that into my head. That we have all got to work together in Mississippi if we're going to do anything about this problem. That happens when either the issue or the problem or something is so overwhelming that you begin to get this consensus and feeling which really overflows any organizational ties and struggles. . . .

PAYNE: Willie Peacock [SNCC organizer in Mississippi] felt that you deliberately did not try to develop yourself as an orator because you had feelings that oratory is not a way necessarily to help people grow.

MOSES: Well, one of the things I felt in Mississippi was that, you always had to understate everything because the problem itself was too big. The problem itself was like immense, so you couldn't go around projecting what you were going to do about the problem, right. What you had to show people was that you were actually biting off a small piece of the problem and you were actually doing that. In Mississippi, when I talked, I just tried to talk about what it was we were doing and tried to emphasize that. I didn't sit down and think this through but my reaction to the situation was, you don't mislead people by promising what you can't deliver or you can't really know what you can deliver because you're dealing now with people who had heard it all, across the years, and seen it just get progressively [worse]. . . . My reaction was to talk only about what we were doing, myself and the little cadre, the people that we had. And, then only to talk really in very specific terms. Like what we're going to do next.

This is what we did over here and now this is what we're going to do this time, here. So, I remember that time, all through that period that, my talk, my speech and everything, was really, sort of, sparse. And I didn't know how any other way to talk there. And you were always afraid that you were going to get people thinking that something was going to happen that wasn't going to happen. You needed people who were, somehow, ready to steel themselves, to be part of what you knew was going to happen, as opposed to promising people something that you knew wasn't going to happen. And we had so few tools. You had the Justice Department, its little Civil Rights Division, John Doar and a couple of lawyers. And then, sort of this little help from these national organizations, but not much. When we had a program, SCLC starts one little program and then we got support from CORE, you know. They sent in a couple of people, support and helping people. And then SNCC, with what it can. That is mainly providing a movement culture for our people to grow up in and mature. That's SNCC's great role, right. That they're really driving the culture for our young people. So, we have a place as we get people attracted to what we're doing that they can grow up in. So, your tools are really your people. Those are your tools, but then the question is, "How do you attract the tools that you need from among these people?" Well, it isn't by getting people who are going to respond to the big speech.

PAYNE: I am jumping back and forth, but in terms of the kinds of people you attracted in the early period in Mississippi one of the things I am struck by is the degree to which so many of them were older people. Do you have a sense of why that was?

MOSES: What seems to me to happen in Mississippi was that you had through the '40s and '50s, you had a generation which grew up in Mississippi and really were battle-scarred by the time we got there. They had been through this, sort of, great isolation, this long battle, and consciously so. That is, there were a group of people there, the NAACP in Mississippi was quite a remarkable collection of people that really had just minimal support. And Medgar [Evers] was remarkable. So you had this collection of people who were going through this struggle and many of them had become wise in the ways . . . of long struggle in which you're surviving and know that you have to keep surviving to keep the struggle growing. And so we fell into all of that. Of course, one of the things their wisdom does is allows them to "read" you. Because their life has depended on reading people. Once they read you and decide that you really are going to work in this struggle that they know only too well, it's like you fall into this whole riches of people. And they pass you along, basically, because they know each other. They pass you along. That's what happens. That's what happened to me. I guess you can say, in a sense, Mississippi created its own executioners.

PAYNE: Marx would have loved it. It's the dialectic worked out perfectly. Why did people stop organizing, I mean stop thinking in that tradition?

MOSES: In the '60s?

PAYNE: Yeah.

MOSES: Within SNCC?

PAYNE: Yeah.

MOSES: Well, first of all, SNCC remember was very young, so its culture was still being formed. The culture, you know, had a lot of different elements in it. So one element, which was very strong, was the nonviolence as a way of life element. That wasn't able to take root in the community. So it didn't really find any real sustenance from the community. So, it's still out there even to this day. . . . But, they haven't found a way to really operationalize that philosophy, other than just in terms of their own personal life. . . . So that was one strong arm. The other which we were part of, dealing with the political empowerment issue and using the vote in trying to delve into the community. The place where it was strongest was Mississippi. That sort of work got turned over to the Freedom Democratic Party. Unfortunately, I think the Freedom Democratic Party, in its leadership did not really, turn to the issue of, "Well how do we do and continue what got us started, which is sort of deepening in our grassroots?" They got, sort of, diverted in questions of national policy in Washington, trying to affect national policy while you may not have enough energy and expertise to do both. So with the leadership going that way and looking that way and the kind of fierce struggle that that got them into, it just zapped the energy. You got pockets where people carried on. But, they didn't have that support. So then within SNCC, you got a movement out of Mississippi, which is sort of the Washing-

ton, D.C. NAG [Nonviolent Action Group] group that Stokely [Car-
michael] assembled. Their reaction to the events of '64, was picking
up and moving to Alabama, to get a place where they could have
some space to work through their own concepts of what they wanted
to do. See, we missed a move there, because we were about this far
away from being able to take [local] Mississippi people to Alabama.
See, if we had been able to keep, sort of, centered on the organizing
aspect and the strategy and everyone agreeing about it. . . . Let me
divert for a second. I think part of the issue is that, in one sense, what
made it an overwhelming problem had been cracked.

PAYNE: The violence?

MOSES: Yes. You had gotten now the national response, which was
going to put to a close the period that we came down to. So, you lost
that consensus. You didn't have that anymore after '64. So people
were now looking for their own ways or for some new consensus.
But, part of what that means is that they're looking for their own idea
of what the next, most important issue is, the most important problem
to work on. So you have some working on this problem: "We'll do
something in Washington." Some working on that problem: "We're
going to go over here in Alabama and we're going to establish a real
party which is not going to be tied to this other stuff up here." You
don't have a strategy to move and carry forward because part of what
you have lost is the consensus. . . .

PAYNE: . . . about what's important.

MOSES: . . . about what's important. Right. And what to do. But, we
were that far away from getting a strategy of now you go to Alabama
but you don't take the organizers to Alabama per se, but you take the
people . . .

PAYNE: . . . from Mississippi who've grown inside the movement.

MOSES: Right. And you now give them their next experience and then
you get a whole different chemistry of what might happen in Alabama. But, Stokely and them, so they go over there. . . .

PAYNE: But you missed that move. Why?

MOSES: Well, you didn't have the concept either within the FDP, 'cause
their attention is diverted to Washington or the SNCC organizers
cause Stokely has got his own idea about what he wants to do. Then
the next step comes when SNCC gets its media figures. That, sort of,
carries the organization out of the mode in which it can really pay

attention to all that. It gets into another mode, which is the mode, which we knew about through King and the other national leaders, which is, you are looking for a media event where you're in this symbiotic relationship with the media. And so, there again, there's only so much energy [and it] gets zapped up into this . . . the actual organizing gets lost. The people in the organizations, it's too much to ask them because they . . . and I saw that early in Mississippi when I began to get some press, then the reaction of the people I was working with, the staff in Mississippi began to shift, to change how they related to me.

PAYNE: Shift in that. . . . What was the reaction?

MOSES: Well the reaction is they are reading about you and so they begin to react to you based on what they read rather than what you had before. Which is you're reacting to people based on your interactions. But, all of a sudden there's this new projection, literature. So, people react to that. It didn't become big enough in Mississippi and we were able to control it and part of the control was that other people, like Mrs. Hamer emerged to take up the media space. Now part of that has to be deliberate. That is, the media space is there and it's got to be taken up so either you've got to sort of hold it vacant until some-one emerges to take it up or you're going to move into it and then get this reaction. . . . Now, part of what happened in the movement was simply, in Mississippi, we really did hold that media space [open], so that it was there when Mrs. Hamer emerged as a person who could fill it and, sort of, deal with the demands of the media. [She was] what they needed. . . . We were talking about this question about what happened to the organizing tradition. So, that's what happened. Stokely got into the media space and there was something in Stokely that wanted to get into that space. Then, when he did that, then he couldn't do what he was doing before. He could no longer organize.

PAYNE: At which I understand he had a real good reputation.

Moses: He was a good organizer. He and his group really played a key role in shaping the delegation which got up to Atlantic City. Because the question was really finding the people. . . .

PAYNE: From the grassroots?

MOSES: Yeah . . . who were going to hold up. When you get up there, you know, who are really going to hold up under pressure, so he did that, his group did.

PAYNE: You were talking about the inability of nonviolence, as a way of life, to root itself in the community and to find a sustaining force. It strikes me that the substance of what I understand them to be saying and the substance of what I understand you to be saying last night when you were talking about your father's humanism, the humanism of a Mrs. Hamer or so on, they seem so close. It's not clear to me why it couldn't be bridged.

Moses: Well, part of the problem is that any kind of philosophy like that, it grows in a certain culture. You can't transport the culture. What moves across cultures is some kernel of the philosophy which can be imbedded in some other culture. So, now you didn't get that with the nonviolent group. You got a term called "Satyagraha," which no one understands and which has meaning in terms of Indian culture. What you had not gotten is sort of a distillation of what the spirit of this is in a way in which it can take wings and be like a seed which gets planted in another culture. . . . But, what's taking root, is something that's been pruned for export. It's sort of been pared down and the essence of some of these things. . . . You go to those workshops and you listen to people talk, there's a mixture in their stuff. Some of it is, sort of, central principles, but then some of it is this other culture which [Black] people are really not into. . . . They're into Jesus and they've been doing Jesus for all these thousands of years or hundreds and hundreds of years and carrying their guns. And so, what they're talking about has got to somehow penetrate that and it never did. . . . It didn't take root. Now, I think it didn't take root within the movement because. . . . The freedom rides brought it into Mississippi and then the issue was will it take root in Mississippi? They tried to do it in Jackson and they failed. That was the summer of '61. Same summer we were in McComb. It's like you had these two different models trying to take root and one did and the other didn't. Now, part of the reason is simply that there is this little sliver, what I later began to think of as a crawl space which is being provided by the '57 Civil Rights Act, which gives you the right [to do voter registration work] . . . really provides a space to crawl in and to organize, so they can't just arrest you. If they do, like they did in Indianola, then the Justice Department is going to step in, so they [advocates of nonviolence] didn't have that, so the whole weight is coming down on them and the civil rights' organizations are saying, "No. Don't come to us for your bail money and stuff." And Jackson is not Nashville, Tennessee so you don't have a Black, middle-class community which is going to support you and those that might are within the NAACP and it's a closed shop; the NAACP is not supporting this activity. And Medgar is viewing us as a sort of threat, so he is not supporting that. They are literally thrown back on themselves. Now, having been thrown back on themselves . . . I don't know what they needed to come up with but they certainly don't come up with, "We're going to stay in jail and watch the support build up around our long-term jail sentences."

PAYNE: Let me go back to Medgar for a second. I know a little bit about his, sort of rejecting all of you at first. Then I guess, he kind of grew into the idea. I am just curious as to how you saw him. You said a moment ago that he was remarkable.

MOSES: Well, you think about it. He's not getting any real support. You read some of his letters that Taylor Branch dug into. He's arguing with Gloster Current [of the National NAACP] about paying for his tires and he's traveling all over the state. He's got his gun on his seat, traveling. He's a marked man and he's got a lot of integrity. This group that we have talked about, they read him and so they are all with Medgar, but they also understand that the national organization is just going to do so much. Really, they're not going to do much maybe send a lawyer in and file something in the court system, which is controlled by the enemy. So, he really is strapped.

PAYNE: And yet he just keeps on. Just keeps on.

Moses: That was his whole life.

PAYNE: It's just not there. A lot of what you just said about Medgar would apply to Amzie [Moore], up in the Delta.

MOSES: Except that Amzie's not working for the NAACP.

PAYNE: He's got that kind of freedom.

MOSES: Yeah. He's not a staff person.

PAYNE: So, he's out there by himself?

MOSES: He's out there by himself. Well, less so than Medgar. Because, Amzie is out there embedded in his network which is deeper than Medgar's, in one sense 'cause Medgar is working, sort of, as a state person. . . . If you're working a whole state, you know, traveling around, then your network is different than if you, you know, work in an area, and . . .

PAYNE: . . . are rooted in that area.

MOSES: You're rooted in that area and your network is going down to people who are not visible, who are not leading the local branch or anything. And so Amzie has a different [support base] and Medgar's handicapped because he is part of the organization and so he's got to think strategy in terms of how does this affect the organization? And Amzie doesn't and has been there long enough and also has been involved in the Delta Council [the Regional Council of Negro Leadership]. He's really looking at this problem. Amzie, is your movement person. He's really asking, What are we going to do? Where are the resources? Where's the energy? And he's always looking, and he sees it in the students. That here's a source of energy that really could impact this problem and you don't want to tie it up within an organizational structure that's really got its head in a certain place.

PAYNE: . . . and just is not going to be moved.

Moses: Right.

PAYNE: You were saying last night that Ella Baker formed one large part of your thoughts, your philosophy of organizing and Amzie the other and we never got a chance to say anything about them. Why don't you elaborate.

MOSES: Ella . . . had a vision about leadership and she would run programs and was trying to create context for leadership and education for leadership. And, sort of, promoting this idea about grassroots leadership and then you saw it at work in how she fought for the space so that SNCC could emerge and SNCC leadership could emerge. On the other hand, Amzie was being a leader and also being an organizer. Amzie operated in two very distinct modes. In Cleveland he was the leader and as some of the movement people found out (laughter) you couldn't breach his leadership in Cleveland. You couldn't cross him and you couldn't try to move around him. In the state, however, he was an organizer and he functioned as an organizer and he worked behind the scenes and worked with other people and so Amzie provided, sort of, some flesh and bones to Ella's theory, into what she was living at this other level. You couldn't experience what Ella was talking about with her in a community. Because she wasn't in a community. She was operating in this network world. Amzie was operating in this community and you could see what she was talking about in this role of leadership and organizing. . . . Now Amzie organized the bus that took the group from Ruleville down to Indianola in '62 [to attempt to register]. He was our launching station. When I first came, he sat me down in McComb and he was not really ready to move. The one thing that I understood . . . there was nothing I could do if Amzie wasn't ready to do it. I didn't try to move. I spent my time, just, sort of, picking up what I could, watching Amzie, going where he told me to go. A lot of it was, "Let's go." You didn't know where you were going before[hand] and you were told where you were going on the way. I think, one of the modes in that kind of situation is you don't—and I picked that up, as I began to work—is you don't telegraph what you're doing. You keep, really, all the information about the movement, how and where you're moving real close and so you don't do a lot of talking about what you're going to do. So now, people who came in, who tried to organize under Amzie, if he didn't want it to happen, it didn't happen. . . .

PAYNE: Another thing you were saying last night about your father. A lot of the people I've heard you talk about, Amzie, Webb Owens, I think, Cleve Jordan in Greenwood. They strike me as working-class intellectuals, C. C. Bryant. . . .

MOSES: Owens was. Webb Owens and Amzie were; C. C.'s a different cut. Cause C. C. Bryant he's, C. C. Bryant really was an organization man. On the one hand, through NAACP and through his work in the union on the railroad. 'Cause his mind was, sort of, locked in, so what you always got from C. C. Bryant, you're always getting the same stories and he's telling them over and over again and never losing any of the excitement or the immediacy of the story. I mean C. C. Bryant is a real folk character and he continues to be one. He's different from Webb Owens. Webb Owens and Amzie really had this analytical turn, and they're turning everything over and looking at it. So you get the ability to look at this stuff through all this prism of experience because it's the analytical turn of mind which has been honed by experience as opposed to by books and educational institutions.

PAYNE: And that describes your father, too, doesn't it? That analytical turn?

MOSES: Yeah. But what is lacking in my father is this exposure to a sustained struggle which has involved a large network of people, not just the struggle of your family and your own personal life and your own personal surroundings.

PAYNE: But on a larger canvass?

MOSES: Yes. Right. So, he didn't have that. His struggle, all his struggles—and that sort of was his weak point, right—because all his struggle was around his own personal life and so the issues that he was struggling with he never got a chance to struggle with them and turn his own personal struggles into this larger struggle and so his personal struggles sort of ate him and he drank as a result of that. That really gave a turn to his life and to his family. It was hard, it was hard on my mother.

PAYNE: On all of you. It was obviously a close family.

MOSES: Right. And so we all. . . . Well, what it means is that we can't count on him. So my mother could never count on him like on holidays . . . Christmas.

PAYNE: Bob, is there anything else about Amzie's impact on you?

MOSES: Well, Amzie had the impact of providing me a home, so I knew that I could turn up any hour of the night, any day of the week. I didn't have to have any money and I was as welcome as a son. I was his son in the movement, so I had a *family* connection. I think that's what sustained me. It was that you were moved into a set of movement families and accepted within these families as a part of their family so C. C. Bryant's family, Steptoe's family, Amzie Moore's family, old man Saunders, Miss Pilcher . . . we had this network. Now, it was an amazing experience 'cause I had never before or since had that experience where you. . . . It's so much literally like you were throwing yourself on people and they have actually picked you up and are going to carry you. So you don't really need money. You don't really need transportation. It may take you a while to get where you need to go . . . but somebody's going to get you where you have to go. You don't really need insurance, because they are going to see that you get your medical needs taken care of and your dental needs taken care of and your food, they're going to see that you eat. And I've never been before or since, in that setting. It's a really liberating kind of experience because you move around and everywhere you move, there is someone there who really has a welcome ready for you. You can show up any time. It doesn't matter. So Amzie was the first of those. We had a lot of time, particularly in the beginning, before I went to McComb, just to talk. He would really just talk and Amzie was walking history, so he knew all of this history, and all of these people, sort of the whole history of the Delta. . . . I got a good grounding, in the sense that what you need, you need a map, someone who lays out what the terrain is and is not doing it abstractly, but is sort of laying it out. He's doing for me what my father did in the personal arena where my father was always telling me about this person and that person and how to understand them, so Amzie is really analyzing and laying out this whole, sort of, cast of characters across the state and really bringing me in on who are the people who are the players and how to work with them and what to expect of this one, what's this one's orientation.

PAYNE: By this time, he'd been at it for fifteen years or more?

MOSES: Since World War II. He's taken me under his wing. He's done a reading [of me.] (Laughter). He's just made a decision.

PAYNE: I want to go back to what you were saying about your father just now. Part of the discussion last night was the idea that part of what predisposes you to be open to what Ella Baker had to say is what you had gotten from your father. You want to just expand on that?

MOSES: Well, when I look at the early influences. . . . Well my father is, sort of, modeling this, on one hand, this acceptance of people, so he has this great capacity to deal with the person that's presented in front of him and sort of see through the various kinds of stereotypes, so he's always dealing with the actual person and then within that also has this capacity willing to look for and respond to human qualities of that person, so he is not predisposed to try to put that person down. So, part of his life, he has this network of people who are part of his personal network. Some are family, on both sides of the family, his side and my mother's side that he's visiting. Then, some are people on his job; he has this job at the 369th Armory and he's had it since the Depression.

PAYNE: And what was the job?

MOSES: Well, the official title is Armorer. Well, what that means is you're, sort of, a person who is providing janitorial services. You're operating a switchboard sometimes. You clean up the snow. . . . So, that's what he's doing, all my life. So, he's got this job . . . up into the '50s. Even when my mother died, he's still working. And, so he has a network through there, the people that he's known and worked with and he has some network through Uncle Bill. I guess a few of his family, through his father and the kind of people who knew his father. And so, some of these people, he's still, sort of networked with. So, as a kid, I traveled with him. I liked to go and listen, so I spent a lot of time listening to adult conversation and what he does, which I think really helps me later on, he's always pointing out to me about the person that we just talked to and what they are, what's real about them or if we meet somebody who he thinks is not real.

PAYNE: He's teaching you how to read [people].

MOSES: That's right. Exactly.

PAYNE: At the same time, teaching you how to listen.

MOSES: Well, he likes to talk, so I don't know if he's teaching me how to listen or I am just listening 'cause he likes to talk. He talks a lot and he likes to talk and he likes to talk about interesting issues. It's not just gossip talk. We're sitting and talking about issues of the day, right. And they may be issues which are related to the job and how it is that you can't really somehow make this job work. And what does it mean 'cause this is a Black unit in the army? And, at some point his brother is the commanding officer 'cause his brother is a lieutenant colonel in the army, his older brother, and so at one point he's actually in the position in that he's the janitor in the building his brother is running. So, he had all these issues and things. And that's part of the thing of his life was looking at life from these different perspectives, so he's here at the bottom, but there are also people who are closely connected with him who have these connections at higher levels, so this idea, sort of looking at the environment in Harlem and the structure and everything from the point of view of the man in the street, I think probably that that affected my whole interest in, attraction to working [at the] grassroots. I think that's coming out of Pop and coming out of my being fascinated with that as a kid.

PAYNE: You were saying that one of the things that impressed you about Ella was how much she was interested in you as a person.

MOSES: I think what I was saying, in part was, this is also part of that culture but a lot of people lose it, so they move up in certain arenas, operating in certain arenas and the sense of importance of what they are or what they are doing, sort of overshadows this culture, which is that you make a personal connection whenever you really want to do something with somebody else. The first thing you have to do is make this personal connection. You've got to find out who it is you're really working with. You really have to be interested in that person, to work with them. That the working begins with that kind of relationship. It's this idea that you just don't work in the abstract. That part of the working with people is making this kind of personal communication the basis for the work, so without that, you can't really, sort of, get off the ground. You saw that all across the South in your grassroots, rural people . . . Ella carried that style into this other level where she's actually doing this kind of organizing work and networking with people and has this wide range of contacts. She was, sort of, shepherding the SNCC kids through all these mazes and part of what she's doing in doing that, she's making part of the initial steps is always making these personal connections with all of them as they come through, and become part of this until it was time for her to leave.

PAYNE: Is it fair to say, that that style of work in which you're trying to take a genuine personal interest as well as develop a political relationship. That withers five to six years later in the movement?

MOSES: Or does the movement wither?

PAYNE: OK . . . I am not sure which is the chicken and which is the egg.

MOSES: Right. You've got this other culture taking over, ministerial culture. Ministers of defense. It's the shell of a political relationship. It's not really a political relationship. It's sort of the facade. You really go off into something else 'cause there's no real power. That's the reason for giving it a title.

NOTE

Thanks to Thomas Rush for his careful transcription of this interview.

DISCUSSION QUESTIONS

1. What assumptions does Moses make about how social change is made?

2. Moses sees the movement as a positive context for youth development. What are the contemporary parallels for such a context? Where do people now get "credentialized"?
3. Judging from this interview, what potentials do you see for conflict between SNCC and other civil rights organizations?
4. What are the advantages of oratory in a mass movement? The disadvantages?

7

AN INTERVIEW WITH
ELDRIDGE W. STEPTOE, JR.

M oses mentions the Steptoe family as one of the important movement families of Mississippi. E. W. Steptoe organized the Amite County branch
of the NAACP in 1954. The fact that he was able to survive in one of the
South's most violent areas may have had something to do with his reputation for
being willing to defend himself. One organizer who stayed with him—as many
did—noted there were "just guns all over the house, under pillows, under chairs.
It was just marvelous." Relatively free from reprisals, landowning families like
the Steptoes were a crucial constituency for the rural movement. In this interview
from the Mississippi Oral History Program of the University of Southern Mississippi, Mr. Steptoe's determination is remembered by his son, Eldridge W. Steptoe, Jr. The interview was conducted in November 1995. The interviewer is
Jimmy Dykes.

STEPTOE: The civil rights movement, as far as I'm concerned and as far
as my family's concerned, it began in the early '50s when my father
saw a need to go to the courthouse in Liberty, Mississippi, to try to
register and be a part of the electoral process. And he was turned
down by the people in the courthouse and told him precisely that
they wouldn't allow him to register and vote just because people in
Amite County didn't let Black people register and vote. And then I
think on another occasion shortly after that he went back again and
sort of insisted. Somebody in the courthouse told him that they
would let him vote since he was a property owner and this kind of
thing, but [they] wouldn't let everybody register and vote. He said,
well, if everybody couldn't register to vote, then he didn't want to
register and vote. He wanted all of his people to be able to register

189

and vote. So shortly after that he made some contact with a national organization, the NAACP. Some people out of New Orleans that had an NAACP branch going. And he established a local chapter of the NAACP in Amite County and began to talk to local people about what his intentions were and what he would like to have done, you know, and telling the people about their rights that were being violated and his desire to be able to register and vote in Amite County. And so they began a meeting, began to have regular meetings at the local church here. Then one night the sheriff and his men in Amite County had found out about the meeting going on down there. And they went down to this church where they were holding the meeting and disrupted the meeting down there and took the books. They had a secretary, president, and all this. They took the books. My father thought that it brought about a need for him to get some more people in here because he didn't think that it was right for them to come in to disrupt a peaceful meeting that they were holding down there. . . . Medgar Evers was still alive at the time. Medgar Evers began to come. He got him to come down to this area to talk to the people in the community, the churches. The people he couldn't get them to meet with him anymore because they was afraid, because the sheriff and his men had kind of threatened them, intimidated the people. And a lot of the Black people owed some debts to various people and they used that, you know, to tell them—when they saw their name on the roster, you know, they would tell them about what could happen and how can you afford to be a member of this NAACP if you owe this person that and this person that. This kind of thing.

DYKES: Excuse me for interrupting, but what did your father do for a living, Mr. Steptoe?

STEPTOE: He was a farmer. We had a cotton farm and a dairy. So after they disrupted the NAACP meeting, then he had to go from house to house. Whenever he would get information or he wanted to talk to them about what steps he was going to take next, he would go from house to house and talk to the people throughout the county. And as things went on he would go to Jackson, Mississippi, to meetings with Medgar Evers and the people in Jackson, gathering information about what could be done and what the other people in the state of Mississippi were doing. But he was having to struggle because the people were afraid to meet. And he would go to churches and talk to church groups, you know, to kind of disrupt the services. And people were very patient with him disrupting the churches, getting a spot on the program to talk to them about the civil rights movement and what he was trying to do. Medgar Evers was able to put him in contact with some more state people involved in the NAACP and also some people on the national level. And he began to make trips to Atlanta and to Washington. And then he got in touch with Bob Moses, and Bob Moses came down and talked to him on several occasions. And then he thought that it would be a good idea for them to set up a voter's registration [project] here in Mississippi to teach people how to register, how to vote, and these kinds of things. And then at this time [1961] all over the state of Mississippi the people had begun to work toward the same kind of thing.

DYKES: What did Mr. Herbert Lee's death do to the movement as far as the work that your father was doing? Did it make people more afraid?

STEPTOE: Well, it intensified the movement in that some of the local people were—it frightened some of the local people. But at that time we had people from outside of the county that were coming in. And it gave support to those people [who] were actively involved in the movement in the local areas. And we also—the Justice Department had been sending people down here. The FBI had been in the area a great deal. So they felt a sense of protection, you know, because of the kind of thing that had been taking place.

DYKES: Well, I've read that even with the FBI and the local police, a lot of times that if Blacks were gathered for any type of meeting that bad things would happen to them and they would not be protected by the FBI or the local police. Did you ever witness any incidents like that?

STEPTOE: I never witnessed that, but that was very true. But for my daddy and some of the people who had hoped and had vowed to go through with this thing regardless of what happened, they felt like they did have some latitude [and] support. Some of the FBI people would come, and my daddy felt comfortable with them, and some would come that he didn't trust. But for the most part the fact that they were here meant a great deal to the movement and to my father as he worked in the movement. But he was very skeptical about everybody that came, except those people who had proven that they really were for their protection and this kind of thing. But, you know, it was very scary during those times for those people who lived here because they didn't know who they could trust. And this is why some of the people just completely withdrew.

DYKES: Well, how hard was it for your father? I know from what I've read and researched [that] as a rule any people that had any dealings with white people, any Black people that had any dealings with white people, if you worked for them or if you owed them money there was so much pressure on them not to get involved in the movement. How much of a force was this for your father to try to influence people that it was for their own good for them to get involved in the movement? Was this a big issue?

STEPTOE: Yes, quite a big issue. Many of the people that lived in this area, however, had their own property. But there were those that lived on plantations. There were few that lived on the plantations that he knew that there would be very little use in talking to them about involving them in this kind of a movement because they [the plantation owners] had control over them and they wouldn't allow them to get involved in anything like this. So therefore, he wasn't able to and he never did—in other words, he wanted to protect those people; so therefore, he wouldn't want them or let them get involved in it because he knew just about what would happen to them. But some of the property owners, some of the Black property owners who had their own property and their own businesses, their own farm, some of those who owed banks or white people, then they were reluctant to be [active] in the movement because they felt that they would make it hard for them, foreclose on them.

DYKES: Well, what about, you know, there were a few occupations where Blacks didn't have any—whites didn't have as much pressure over them, for instance ministers. . . . Do you think that your father got the support from the local ministers that he should have or could have?

STEPTOE: No, he wasn't able to secure the kind of support from the ministers that he thought that he should have gotten. I recall at one church he went to and asked for permission to be on the agenda, on the program of the church and they denied him. And he would ask for certain announcements to be read about meetings and these kind of things and they wouldn't do that.

DYKES: Did they give him a reason for not . . .

STEPTOE: Nothing except they were afraid. Because during those times they were burning churches in the three-county area and they were afraid of that and afraid that something would happen to them personally. They just felt like it wasn't safe for that congregation, I guess. He got teed off with all the ministers in the area except the one here in the local community in our church [Mount Pilgrim Baptist Church]. But, you know, he kind of made the decision as to what would happen in this church down here, my daddy did, so that was no problem. But the other churches in the area, he didn't get the kind of support from the preachers. He felt like you know that they didn't have any kind of a backbone. And some of the local people that, like I said, that had property and all, he was kind of—well, he understood the reason why some of the people was afraid. He didn't give them a hard time for it. There were a few people that weren't afraid that went with him, that was only two or three. But most of the people who he would contact, he'd have to go to their house at night and contact the people. They didn't want to be seen with him. They didn't want to be seen talking to him. Even if he would meet some of his friends or people on the streets in town or someplace, they would kind of duck. They didn't want to talk to him because they felt like the white people would see him talking to them and they'd put them in the same category and this kind of thing. So it was very, very hard on him, but he was persistent enough to continue, and he didn't stop. And he wasn't afraid of anything.

DYKES: Was the NAACP the only organization that he was a member of?

STEPTOE: No, he was a member of the other organizations that came about as a result of the movement. SNCC [Student Nonviolent Coordinating Committee] and CORE [Congress for Racial Equality] . . . and COFO [Council of Federated Organizations]. Yeah, that was, COFO was in McComb. That was where they had an organization of people there that had a building there on Summit Street, I believe. And we had a direct—see, my daddy couldn't get a telephone down here, so that he had to get a short wave radio system. He was able to communicate with—see, because our house had been turned into a

base, an office like, and they had a COFO base set up there in Mc-
Comb. So in order to be able to communicate daily with them, they
wouldn't give us a telephone, so he had to get a short wave radio
system, and they communicated on the radio system. Yeah. . . . We
had the station down here we called mike base at our house, but we
had the system set up down there. The movement became wide
open. And the people began to work hard in it when more women
got involved in it. Because when it was just the NAACP and my
daddy and the men, well, after these things happened with these law
enforcement who came down, then it was hard for him to get [them]
back. And he had to go by himself from house to house and these
kind of things. So finally he started going from church to church, and
women began following him, and then that kind of opened up the
movement. And then when people started coming down, coming in
from [out of town and out of state] to support the movement, then
that gave him [more] latitude and it became very effective, more
effective because more people were involved and more people who
could work that he could depend on and get more done that way.
Because these [out of town] people who came in, they weren't afraid
of anything, even though some of their people were getting killed
and these kind of things. They didn't stop.

DYKES: Were any of those students [from the north] involved in the
Liberty area to help voter registration?

STEPTOE: Yes. Bob Moses made some contacts somewhere in the north
and placed articles in the paper about what was going on down here,
that there was an old man down here in Amite County that was
struggling, trying to do something about the injustices that exist down
here for Black people. And people began to volunteer to come down
and support the movement that was taking place. And quite a number
of them came. Many of them lived here in Amite County with my
daddy. My daddy opened up his house to about five or six of the
workers, and they were in and out all day every day and all night
long, you see. And the kind of thing that needed to be done, they
were there to help and they did a good job.

DYKES: Were there any repercussions on your dad as far as—I know in
the McComb area a lot of the people that housed some of the workers
and stuff, you know, they had things bad things that happened to
them. Was that as frequent in this area?

STEPTOE: No, we didn't have any problems with that. Maybe sometime when some of the workers, they would see some of the workers going back and forward, somebody might heckle them or something or say something ugly, but they didn't pay any attention. But it wasn't a factor at all down here, because, you know, we were so thin down here and there wasn't very much activity going on in this area. The activities that they were participating in down here [dealt with] getting registered and [voting]. And once the civil rights [legislation] passed, then there was a [need to] get people together, [to organize] people and [to set] up centers all over the county, to get people to communicate and to talk and to work together and to teach children and young adults, you know, what it is that they're supposed to be doing and how not to be afraid to go to the [polling] place and register and vote and how to sustain yourself once you become a registered person [with the ability] to vote. Because that was one of the things that we were afraid of. And it has happened, people haven't utilized the rights that they secured in a way that is in the best interest of all of the people.

DYKES: What do you mean by that, Mr. Steptoe?

STEPTOE: Well, before the Black people were able to register and vote, well, they had no power, and the people that were running for office didn't [pay attention to] them too much because they didn't have any power, they didn't have any voting power. But then once they began to register and vote, then the other people changed their strategies, began to . . .

DYKES: Redistricting and . . .

STEPTOE: Yeah, redistricting and then telling them how to vote (pounds on table) and promising them things in order for them to vote in the way they wanted them to vote, you know. So you can see evidence of it now, that many of the people who are voting now they are voting, many of them, are voting the way that some of the candidates want them to vote because they have promised them this or they have promised them that, these kind of things. I just feel bad about that because this is not the kind of thing that the people who died for this right envisioned taking place.

DYKES: Well, you would have to agree that a lot of progress has been made, though, maybe not as much as you would like. But just in Pike County there's a Black man, the seventh of November, in this election, is in the runoff for sheriff. And there are several other elected officials that are Black. Are you satisfied with the progress or . . .

STEPTOE: . . . But yes, you're going to get Black people elected here [and there]. I think the state of Mississippi has more Black [elected officials] than any other state, I believe. But that's beside the point. The point is that the needs of the people, the needs of the county, the needs of the local [citizens]—what I mean is that the people within these counties, need to be able to elect people that can do the best job for them, and that's not getting done. It's the most popular people and not necessarily the people that are most capable. You know, I guess I'm a little idealistic, but that kind of thing bothers me a great deal. And I think the [purpose of the] civil rights movement was for Black people to be able to participate in the electoral process, and to maintain the kind of, I wouldn't say power, but maintain the kind of strength that it takes to put the right kind of people in the right kind of position to make things better. I don't mean to give Black people this or give Black people that but in dealing honestly and [fairly] with all people. I think the boat has been missed to a certain degree, you know, on the part of white people and on the part of the Black people also.

STEPTOE: Yes. But back to the movement, I thought that the fact that Black people in the '50s and '60s were isolated, systematically excluded from things, was the thing that caused E. W. Steptoe to work for civil rights, to work in the civil rights movement or get involved in the civil rights movement and to bring about the kind of things that had happened in Amite County and throughout the state and the country. He used to read the paper all the time before this thing happened. He used to read the paper all the time looking for and pulling for certain people to be elected. But it was an empty feeling, he used to say. It was an empty feeling to read the paper and hope that this person would get elected and that person would get elected. Maybe he'll make things better. He just kept wishing [that] every president [who] was elected, "Maybe he'll make things better for this county. Maybe he will help us down here." But nobody was able to do anything. I remember one day when the principal of my high school came to my classroom and said that there's a NAACP meeting going to be held in the community at a lodge hall. He wanted the children to tell their parents to be present. In the dairy that evening when I mentioned to my daddy that Mr. Crowley said that there was going to be a meeting held tonight and the attorneys from New Orleans were going to be there for this NAACP meeting, his eyes got [big and bright]. He just dropped everything he was doing and told me, "Y'all finish this, I'm going." And he went. That's where he got his charter from [the organization] to organize and to see what it was like. I think he went to two meetings. And that's when he [formed] this chapter up here and got the people together and they started off. And that's where that fight started; that's where the thing started. And it grew and it grew until he became one of the Freedom Democratic Party [representatives] from Amite County in 1968, I believe. When [the Democratic National Convention] was [in Atlantic City], New Jersey, he was the member of the [Mississippi delegation] that unseated the regulars. I don't know if you remember that. Yeah, well, he was in the Mississippi delegation that went to the Democratic National Convention that year. But that was a long struggle. It took a lot out of him. . . . [When the Voting Rights Act of 1965] passed [he] felt like it was a sense of achievement because he wanted to—he said several times right after that, he said, "Well, I just want to see one election where Black people are going to the polls and voting without being intimidated. And we'll have Black poll watchers as well as white poll watchers standing at the same poll, and Black people and white people going in there and voting for who they feel is the best person for this kind of job." And then the second year the people got around to him and asked him to run for office. He ran for representative of this district. And he lost, but he made a real good run. And he said that he was so elated and so happy to see the people going out to register and vote until he said that he was ready to die then.

DISCUSSION QUESTIONS

1. What factors determine who gets into "history," who gets remembered?
2. What do you suppose it would have been like to be a child growing

up in the Steptoe family? How would it have been different if the activist parent were the mother rather than the father?

3. Visit an online oral history collection. (The Center for Oral History and Cultural Heritage at the University of Southern Mississippi has a very good one: www.usm.edu/oralhistory/) What are the advantages and disadvantages of oral histories as a way to recall the past?

8

AN INTERVIEW WITH
FANNIE LOU HAMER

A sharecropper and farm laborer most of her life, Fannie Lou Hamer became the best-known face of the grassroots movement in the South. In this interview, conducted in 1972 by Neil McMillen for the Mississippi Oral History Program of the University of Southern Mississippi, Mrs. Hamer reflects on the harshness of her youth, her first attempts to register, and conditions in her hometown of Ruleville, Mississippi in the early 1970s. Mrs. Hamer died in 1977.

McMILLEN: Mrs. Hamer, why don't we begin with something about your childhood life? Where were you born and what was your life like when you were a little girl?

HAMER: Well, I was born fifty-four years ago on a plantation in the hills, the kind of place that's something similar to Hattiesburg, the place where you are from. In fact I was the last child of twenty children, six girls and fourteen boys. I'm the twentieth child of a very poor family, sharecroppers [who] never had anything—family life. [We] didn't hardly have food to eat.

My family moved to Sunflower County when I was two years old; that's fifty-two years ago [that] they moved here to Sunflower County, so I was mostly raised here in the Delta. In fact, from two years old up until now I've been in the Delta. My family moved here, and we moved on a plantation; the landowner was named Mr. E. W. Brandon. So we lived on his place until I was grown, but it was just hard. Life was very hard; we never hardly had enough to eat; we didn't have clothes to wear. We had to work real hard, because I started working when I was about six years old. I didn't have a chance to go to school too much, because school would only last about four months at the time when I was a kid going to school. Most of the time we didn't have clothes to wear to that [school]; and then if any work would come up that we would have to do, the parents would take us out of the school to cut stalks and burn stalks or work in dead lands or things like that. It was just really tough as a kid when I was a child.

McMILLEN: What subjects did you like when you were in school, Mrs. Hamer?

HAMER: I loved reading when I was in school. When I was a child, I loved to read. In fact, I learned to read real well when I was going to school. I never had a chance to go to school too long—about six years—but I believe I can compete today with a kid now that's twelfth grade at least.

McMILLEN: So how did you spend your life then from when you were finished with your six years of school?

HAMER: Well, that was just in and out of school—in and out of school, until I was grown. I'd just have some months I'd be in school and some I wouldn't.

McMILLEN: Then you worked, of course?

HAMER: Yes.

McMILLEN: Did you work in the fields?

HAMER: Yes, I worked in the fields. In fact, all the kids around in this Delta worked in the fields. Wasn't no other work to do. They didn't have no such thing as factories; these factories are something new. They didn't have any factories; wasn't nothing to do but fieldwork. That's all you had to do, though. This time of year, well, when there was no cotton to chop, we would be raking corn stalks or doing something like this. But there was never, never a time in April that kids would be in school when I was a kid—never a time that a kid would be in school in April.

McMILLEN: Of course, not at all in the summer.

HAMER: Not at all in the summer. But they worked because there was much more work to do at that time than there is now because they don't let the people work in the fields now. But at that time you didn't get nothing for it, but you could work steady, because when the cotton got up big enough to chop, you—we called it "hoeing the cotton," because it wasn't chopping. After you hoed the cotton about two or three times, then you would call what they called chopping because it wouldn't be bad then. We would just go over it from three to four, sometimes five times. I remember during the time I was a kid, and since I've been grown, some people would be in the front with the hoe chopping cotton, and the other people would be behind them in about a week with a sack picking cotton. They just worked from one season to the other one. There wasn't no such thing as a period where they had a lapse between there. They just chopped cotton, chopped cotton, over and over. When they'd go over it one time, if they finished up about Monday, sometimes they'd have a week out, and then they'd be right back in the field and go over that cotton again. They would keep doing that, and then when time came to harvest the crops, there wouldn't be grass and stuff in it. They could pick it, and it would be clean because it wouldn't be like it is now; they use chemicals and all that. But they didn't use chemicals then; people used hoes to clean that cotton out.

McMillen: Let's move forward in time, Mrs. Hamer. When was the first time you really wanted to vote?

Hamer: That was 1962.

McMillen: Tell us about your efforts to vote.

Hamer: Well, I didn't know anything about voting; I didn't know any- thing about registering to vote. One night I went to the church. They had a mass meeting. And I went to the church, and they talked about how it was our right, that we could register and vote. They were talking about we could vote out people that we didn't want in office, we thought that wasn't right, that we could vote them out. That sounded interesting enough to me that I wanted to try it. I had never heard, until 1962, that Black people could register and vote.

McMillen: When you first tried to vote, where was that? Was that in Ruleville?

Hamer: When I first tried to register?

McMillen: Yes ma'am.

Hamer: Well, when I first tried to register it was in Indianola. I went to Indianola on the 31st of August in 1962; that was to try to register. When we got there—there was eighteen of us went that day—so when we got there, there were people there with guns and just a lot of strange looking people to us. We went on in the circuit clerk's office, and he asked us what did we want; and we told him what we wanted. We wanted to try to register. He told us that all of us would have to get out of there except two. So I was one of the two persons that remained inside, to try to register, [with] another young man named Mr. Ernest Davis. We stayed in to take the literacy test. So the registrar gave me the sixteenth section of the Constitution of Mississippi. He pointed it out in the book and told me to look at it and then copy it down just like I saw it in the book: Put a period where a period was supposed to be, a comma and all of that. After I copied it down he told me right below that to give a real reasonable interpretation then, interpret what I had read. That was impossible. I had tried to give it, but I didn't even know what it meant, much less to interpret it.

McMILLEN: Lawyers don't know what it means.

HAMER: Well, I didn't know.

McMILLEN: So what happened then? You were arrested, weren't you?

HAMER: Well, when we got started back to Ruleville, we were stopped by a state highway patrolman and the city police, and they ordered us to get off of the bus. We got off of the bus, and then they told us to get back on the bus and go back to Indianola. We got back on the bus and we went back to Indianola. When we got back to Indianola, they arrested one of the men that was with us, which was Mr. Lawrence Guyot. They arrested him, and then they told this man who'd drove us down there that his bus had too much yellow on it. They fined him a hundred dollars, but they finally cut his fine down to thirty dollars. We got enough to pay his fine and come on into Ruleville.

McMILLEN: But you didn't spend time in jail that time?

HAMER: I didn't go to jail even, that time. We just went back. It was just one of the people arrested and that was the man that was with us.

McMILLEN: Now let's go back a little bit to when you first heard about voting. Was that Mr. Robert Moses and the Student Nonviolent Coordinating Committee people?

HAMER: That's right.

McMILLEN: I see. He [Moses] was there in person, that's where you [met him]?

HAMER: I was with them on the bus the day that we went down to register.

McMILLEN: With Robert Moses?

HAMER: That's right.

McMILLEN: Now when you heard about it first, though, in the school-house back before you tried to register, when you first heard about voting . . .

HAMER: At the church?

McMILLEN: Yes, at church. Did you hear it from Robert Moses?

HAMER: I heard it from Robert Moses and another man named Jim Foreman. He was from the Student Nonviolent Coordinating Committee. He told us that we had a right. There was another man from CORE, Congress of Racial Equality, and his name was David Dennis. All of them talked about it that night, and after they talked about it, it just made enough sense to me that I wanted to try it.

McMILLEN: Did he tell you it might be dangerous in Mississippi to try to vote?

HAMER: They didn't tell us that it might be dangerous.

McMILLEN: Did you think it was dangerous that first time you tried?

HAMER: I had a feeling that [it was]; I don't know why, but I just had a feeling because the morning I left home to go down to register I carried some extra shoes and a bag because I said, "If I'm arrested or anything, I'll have some extra shoes to put on." So I had a feeling something might happen; I just didn't know. I didn't know it was going to be as much involved as it finally was. But I had a feeling that we might be arrested.

McMILLEN: What happened when you got back? Did anything at all happen? Did you lose your home?

HAMER: Well, when we got back I went on out to where I had been staying for eighteen years, and the landowner had talked to my husband and told him I had to leave the place. My little girl, the child that I raised, met me and told me that the landowner was mad and I might have to leave. So during the time that my husband was talking about it, I was back in the house. The landowner drove up and asked him had I made it back. He [my husband] told him I had. I got up and walked out on the porch, and he [told] me did Pap tell me what he said. I told him, "He did." He said, "Well, I mean that, you'll have to go down and withdraw your registration, or you'll have to leave this place." I didn't call myself saying nothing smart, but I couldn't understand it. I answered the only way I could and told him that I didn't go down there to register for him; I went down there to register for myself. This seemed like it made him madder when I told him that.

MCMILLEN: So you had to leave right away?

HAMER: I had to leave that same night.

MCMILLEN: Your husband stayed on to finish the crop?

HAMER: He stayed on because he [landowner] told him the next morning that if he left he wouldn't give us any of our belongings. But if he'd help him harvest the crop, well, he'd give us the rest of our things.

HAMER: Well, after coming back to Ruleville, I went to Tallahatchie County and stayed awhile. After my husband got so frightened, I went to Tallahatchie County and stayed awhile. When I came back, we moved here in Ruleville to 626 East Lafayette Street. We moved in on the 3rd of December, and I went back on the 4th of December to take the literacy test again.

MCMILLEN: Nineteen sixty-two?

HAMER: Nineteen sixty-two, on the 4th of December. That was one Monday. And the registrar gave me another section of the Constitution. [It] was the 49th section of the Constitution of Mississippi, dealing with the house of representatives. He told me to copy that down and to give a reasonable interpretation. I copied that, but we had got hold of [a copy] of the Constitution of Mississippi and had been able to study it. Some of the people from the Student Nonviolent Coordinating Committee would help us to try to interpret it, so that time I gave a reasonable enough interpretation. When I went back to see about it in January, I had passed that literacy test. So I didn't take the test but twice.

MCMILLEN: I see. So then you voted. When did you first vote?

HAMER: Well, the first attempt that I tried to vote I didn't really get to vote. I went up to vote—that was in a primary election because it was in August. We went up to vote that day, and I didn't have two poll tax receipts. I hadn't been paying poll tax, and I didn't have two prior years. They told me I couldn't vote because I didn't have two poll tax receipts.

MCMILLEN: Talk about your activities as a voter registration worker in the early period.

HAMER: Well, it was rough because we would go to places, go in to do voter registration in places, and we talked to people. We would walk the streets in different little areas, and we would tell them we were coming back the next day. And by the next day somebody would be done got to them, and they wouldn't want to talk with us, and this kind of stuff. Some days it would be disgusting, some very disappointing. Some very disappointing. Then we'd go to churches, and occasionally along, they was burning up churches. These are the kinds of things we faced.

McMILLEN: Who would get to the people you talked to?

HAMER: Well, you know, like the landowners. The white people would get to them, and then they would tell them. We would work on them with food, too. We were trying to get people to get commodities; all of that went together, because at that point it was really rough.

McMILLEN: What about the Citizens' Council? What activity did they pursue to prevent you from voter registration, or weren't they active then?

HAMER: Well, they was active. Of course, we couldn't tell what group was doing what. We just knew we would be harassed, and we knew cars would be passing the house loaded with white men, and trucks would be passing there with guns hanging up in the back. They would walk the streets sometimes with dogs. And we knew it was something, but we didn't know what group it was.

McMILLEN: It's been said that most or many SNCC workers, and many COFO workers, too, thought that the Justice Department under Bobby Kennedy was going to offer protection for civil rights workers and voting rights workers. Did you have that understanding, that the people from the Justice Department would keep the white police and the Klansmen and the Council people away and offer protection during your voting rights efforts?

HAMER: I thought that, but we never did get no protection. You know, we would file suits when people would be harassed to go to jail. We'd go in the court and all of that, but nobody was never really—but the FBI. I guess you know about them, too. That was the only people they would send in [to] investigate something, after something be done happened.

McMILLEN: I know about the FBI, but for the record, was the FBI the friend of the Black people, or would you say they were more the friend of the white establishment?

HAMER: I feel like they were more of a friend to the white establishment than they were to the Black people. I still feel that way.

McMILLEN: You still feel that way. But originally, you thought as a voter worker that Justice would offer some support or some help and that John Doar or Mr. [Burke] Marshall. . . .

HAMER: Yes, in fact, we'd get in touch with the Justice Department, Mr. John Doar, and the attorney general at that time was Senator [Robert] Kennedy. I really believed that—I believed with all my heart—that they would protect you. Until a certain length of time. So much went on that nothing was done about, and I had a kind of little leery feeling: Would they really protect us or not? But that didn't stop us from doing what we felt that we had to do.

McMILLEN: Yes. Among yourselves, how did you explain the reluctance of the federal government to come in and support you in your efforts to get your rights as a citizen of the United States?

HAMER: Well, we would just talk about it among ourselves, and some of them would finally just give up on it and say there wasn't nothing going to be done. That's when I've seen a lot of people, Black young people and white young people, become disgusted and disillusioned with the whole setup, you know. They said, "There ain't nobody going to do nothing," and all of that.

HAMER: You know how it was in 1964. Though last night I kind of— couldn't hardly believe it. I went to a parent and teachers conference last night. And there was a large-size group of whites, right in the middle of Central High—a Black principal—there sitting down to-gether. It showed that it can be done. And it was small children there, and it was grown children there, and the parents was out there last night. So, I do know if this country, if they would just, you know, if they would leave the kids alone it would be a lot better. It would be a lot better. These kids have got to be taught to hate!

HAMER: And there are always going to be a few of those standing out there and say, "That's right and I'm not going to do any different." Just like it is here at Ruleville schools. Now, I'm not saying that everybody around Ruleville and Sunflower County goes to Ruleville schools, but it's quite a few parents that's there and was with their kids last night. They had sent this letter out for all the parents to come, and teachers were going to meet, to have a conference, to ask questions, to visit their rooms, talk to the teachers. And I think that was really good.

McMILLEN: What has happened in the Ruleville schools? Have most of the white children . . .

HAMER: Left.

McMILLEN: They've left and been . . .

HAMER: Most of them have left.

McMILLEN: Are some coming back now?

HAMER: Some, I believe, are coming back. I hadn't seen, I've never seen that many parents, white parents, at a PTA meeting.

McMILLEN: Well. But do planters [in 1972] tell their Black hands, "Don't register." Do they say that anymore?

HAMER: I don't think they tell them that anymore. I really don't think they tell them that.

McMILLEN: People aren't afraid then?

HAMER: They're not afraid. They're really not afraid—not of the land-owners telling them that now. I haven't heard nothing like that in a long time.

McMILLEN: Nobody gets arrested or shot at or things like that?

HAMER: No, that hasn't happened in a long time. It's been quite a while. They're having a school trouble up at Drew.

McMILLEN: Yes. What about white officials who manipulate the Black voter? Do whites take advantage of illiterate Blacks in the polling booths?

HAMER: They do!

McMILLEN: How does that work?

HAMER: So help me they do!

McMILLEN: Well, how does it work?

HAMER: Like some of the kids that we had poll watching have seen them just taking ballots, stuffing them, where there wasn't a machine, just stuff them in the box when they came out. There is just no way in the world that you can handle [that].

McMILLEN: This is evidence that things have changed in Mississippi—

the fact that Blacks aren't intimidated anymore when they try to register.

HAMER: No, they're not intimidated.

McMILLEN: How else have they changed in the last, well, seven or eight years? You've seen incredible changes, I think.

HAMER: I've seen incredible change, some of it, some people really are trying to make the change. Some of them is rats, thoroughbred rats, would do the same thing they done in 1964 or '63. But they've got sense enough to realize what power means, and they've got sense enough to know that people can move them with the vote. That means make them act sometime what they really are not. You know, I've seen some of the fishiest things happen in the past two years in this town that I've ever seen. But the guy, when you meet him, he's got a big smile on him and you just think he's almost a saint. But you know he's doing some tricky things. And that's the kind of stuff; they're doing a lot of.

McMILLEN: People haven't changed their minds, they've just changed their outward behavior. Is that it?

HAMER: That's right, that's right. Now, I've seen, with some people, I've seen the change. I never will forget, there's one man in this town was about as worse as anybody I've ever met. And he changed. Now, I couldn't say that for a bunch of them, but I watched that man change.

McMILLEN: What about the Citizens' Council? Is it active anymore?

HAMER: It's probably active because right up there on the highway, on 49, they've got a mecca. Of course it's been almost burned down. And I was just laughing one day, we were going up the highway, and I said that's funny, they didn't allow no Black folks around then and they might get a Black cook, but you couldn't get nothing about as far as going in that place. But the other day they had Black folks repairing the place. What it means, regardless of what they do or how they act, we really need each other. You know, a lot of folks say, "I can make it with them." We got to have each other and they know that, but they hate to admit it. They hate to think to themselves that they need us. But you know, if some of us wasn't in that Black school, you know, that integrated school they call it, they couldn't get all the federal money. So, they need us. That's what happens. It's not all these people, it's some of them—well, there's some I didn't even know about have wished me well through the whole fight. Like a guy came here and he was sick—and that's been about a year ago—but anyway, my husband had to help him up the steps, an old man. And he came to the table on Christmas Day, and he thanked me for what I was doing, said he really appreciated what I was doing. Well, you wouldn't have looked for that from a man that old. Then later on he stopped and asked me did I read Reader's Digest and I told him I did. He said, "Well, you know, I'm having a year's subscription mailed." Now, he's saying what he feels. He appreciated me doing what he was afraid to do. There ain't no telling how many sleepless nights he slept not wanting things to be like they had been all the time. So, that's the price for freedom, too. He is not free until I am free.

McMILLEN: It liberates both.

HAMER: Yes, as I liberate myself, I liberate him.

DISCUSSION QUESTIONS

1. How are the consequences of the movement likely to be different in a small town like Ruleville?
2. How would you explain the less than supportive stance of the FBI?
3. What options did a youth growing up on a plantation in the 1940s have for escaping sharecropping?
4. Take any contemporary major media story, domestic or international. What would it mean to tell that story from the top-down? What would be the major points of emphasis? What would it mean to reframe the same story as a bottom-up story? What are the trade-offs?

SELECTED READINGS

Ball, Howard, Dale Krane, and Thomas P. Lauth. *Compromised Compliance: Implementation of the 1965 Voting Rights Act*. Westport, Conn.: Greenwood Press, 1982.

Beals, Melba Pattillo. *Warriors Don't Cry*. New York: Pocket Books, 1994.

Belfrage, Sally. *Freedom Summer*. Charlottesville: University Press of Virginia, 1990.

Belknap, Michael. *Federal Law and Southern Order: Racial Violence and Constitutional Conflict in the Post-Brown Era*. Athens: University of Georgia Press, 1987.

Berman, William C. *The Politics of Civil Rights in the Truman Administration*. Columbus: University of Ohio Press, 1970.

Biondi, Martha. *To Stand and Fight: The Struggle for Civil Rights in Postwar New York City*. Cambridge, Mass.: Harvard University Press, 2003.

Branch, Taylor. *Parting the Waters: America in the King Years, 1954–63*. New York: Simon & Schuster, 1988.

Brauer, Carl. *John F. Kennedy and the Second Reconstruction*. New York: Columbia University Press, 1977.

Burk, Robert F. *The Eisenhower Administration and Black Civil Rights*. Knoxville: University of Tennessee Press, 1984.

Burns, Stewart, ed. *Daybreak of Freedom: The Montgomery Bus Boycott*. Chapel Hill: University of North Carolina Press, 1997.

Carson, Clayborne. *In Struggle: SNCC and the Black Awakening of the 1960s*. Cambridge, Mass.: Harvard University Press, 1981.

Chafe, William H. *Civilities and Civil Rights: Greensboro, North Carolina, and the Black Freedom Struggle*. New York: Oxford University Press, 1981.

Chappell, David L. *A Stone of Hope: Prophetic Religion and the Death of Jim Crow*. Chapel Hill: University of North Carolina Press, 2004.

Cluster, Dick. *They Should Have Served That Cup of Coffee*. Boston: South End Press, 1979.

Colburn, David R. *Racial Change and Community Crisis: St. Augustine, Florida, 1877–1980*. New York: Columbia University Press, 1985.

Cone, James. *Martin and Malcolm and America: A Dream or a Nightmare?* Maryknoll, N.Y.: Orbis, 1991.

Crawford, Vicki L., Jacqueline Anne Rouse, and Barbara Woods, eds. *Women in the Civil Rights Movement: Trailblazers and Torchbearers, 1941–1965*. Brooklyn: Carlson Publishing, 1990.

D'Emilio, John. *Lost Prophet: The Life and Times of Bayard Rustin*. New York: Free Press, 2003.

Dittmer, John. *Local People: The Struggle for Civil Rights in Mississippi*. Urbana: University of Illinois Press, 1994.

Eskew, Glenn T. *But for Birmingham: The Local and National Movements in the Civil Rights Struggle*. Chapel Hill: University of North Carolina Press, 1997.

Evers, Myrlie B. *For Us, the Living*. New York: Doubleday, 1967.

Fairclough, Adam. *Race and Democracy: The Civil Rights Struggle in Louisiana, 1915–1972*. Athens: University of Georgia Press, 1995.

———. *To Redeem the Soul of America: The Southern Christian Leadership Conference and Martin Luther King, Jr.* Athens: University of Georgia Press, 1987.

Fleming, Cynthia G. *Soon We Will Not Cry: The Liberation of Ruby Doris Smith Robinson*. Lanham, Md.: Rowman & Littlefield, 1998.

Garrow, David J. *Bearing the Cross: Martin Luther King, Jr., and the Southern Christian Leadership Conference*. New York: William Morrow, 1986.

———. *The FBI and Martin Luther King, Jr.* New York: Norton, 1981.

Graham, Hugh Davis. *The Civil Rights Era: Origins and Development of National Policy, 1960–1972*. New York: Oxford University Press, 1998.

Grant, Joanne. *Ella Baker: Freedom Bound*. New York: John Wiley, 1998.

King, Mary. *Freedom Song: A Personal Story of the 1960s Civil Rights Movement*. New York: William Morrow, 1987.

Klarman, Michael J. *From Jim Crow to Civil Rights: The Supreme Court and the Struggle for Racial Equality*. New York: Oxford University Press, 2004.

Kluger, Richard. *Simple Justice: The History of Brown v. Board of Education and Black America's Struggle for Equality.* New York: Vintage, 1975.

Korstad, Robert Rogers. *Civil Rights Unionism: Tobacco Workers and the Struggle for Democracy in the Mid-Twentieth-Century South.* Chapel Hill: University of North Carolina Press, 2003.

Kotz, Nick. *Judgment Days: Lyndon Baines Johnson, Martin Luther King, Jr., and the Laws that Changed America.* Boston: Houghton Mifflin, 2005.

Lau, Peter. *Democracy Rising: South Carolina and the Fight for Black Equality in America since 1865.* Lexington: University of Kentucky Press, 2006.

Lawson, Steven F. *Civil Rights Crossroads: Nation, Community, and the Black Freedom Struggle.* Lexington: University of Kentucky Press, 2003.

———. *In Pursuit of Power: Southern Blacks and Electoral Politics, 1965–1982.* New York: Columbia University Press, 1985.

———. *Black Ballots: Voting Rights in the South, 1944–1969.* New York: Columbia University Press, 1976.

Lewis, John, and Michael D'Orso. *Walking with the Wind: A Memoir of the Movement.* New York: Simon & Schuster, 1998.

McDonald, Laughlin. *A Voting Rights Odyssey: Black Enfranchisement in Georgia.* Cambridge: Cambridge University Press, 2003.

Meier, August, and Elliott Rudwick. *CORE: A Study of the Civil Rights Movement, 1942–1968.* New York: Oxford University Press, 1973.

Mills, Kay. *This Little Light of Mine: The Life of Fannie Lou Hamer.* New York: Dutton, 1993.

Moody, Anne. *Coming of Age in Mississippi.* New York: Dial, 1968.

Morris, Aldon D. *The Origins of the Civil Rights Movement: Black Communities Organizing for Change.* New York: Free Press, 1984.

Norrell, Robert Jefferson. *Reaping the Whirlwind: The Civil Rights Movement in Tuskegee.* New York: Vintage, 1986.

Olson, Lynn. *Freedom's Daughters: The Unsung Heroes of the Civil Rights Movement from 1830–1970.* New York: Scribner, 2001.

O'Reilly, Kenneth. *"Racial Matters": The FBI's Secret File on Black America, 1960–1972.* New York: Free Press, 1989.

Parker, Frank M. *Black Votes Count: Political Empowerment in Mississippi after 1965.* Chapel Hill: University of North Carolina Press, 1990.

Payne, Charles M. *I've Got the Light of Freedom: The Organizing Tradition and the Mississippi Freedom Struggle.* Berkeley: University of California Press, 1995.

Powledge, Fred. *Free at Last? The Civil Rights Movement and the People Who Made It.* New York: Harper, 1991.

Robnett, Belinda. *How Long? How Long? African-American Women in the Struggle for Civil Rights.* New York: Oxford University Press, 1997.

Thernstrom, Abigail M. *Whose Votes Count? Affirmative Action and Minority Voting Rights.* Cambridge, Mass.: Harvard University Press, 1987.

Thornton, Mills. *Dividing Lines: Municipal Politics and the Struggle for Civil Rights in Montgomery, Birmingham, and Selma.* Tuscaloosa: University of Alabama Press, 2002.

Whelan, Charles, and Barbara Whelan. *The Longest Debate: A Legislative History of the 1964 Civil Rights Act.* New York: New American Library, 1986.

Wofford, Harris. *Of Kennedys and Kings: Making Sense of the Sixties.* New York: Farrar, Straus and Giroux, 1980.

X, Malcolm, and Alex Haley. *Autobiography of Malcolm X.* New York: Ballantine, 1992 [1965].

Youth of the Rural Organizing and Cultural Center. *Minds Stayed on Freedom: The Civil Rights Struggle in the Rural South, an Oral History.* Boulder, Colo.: Westview, 1991.

ACKNOWLEDGMENTS

The documents following the chapters were reprinted from the following sources.

To Secure These Rights: The Report of the President's Committee on Civil Rights. Washington, D.C.: U.S. Government Printing Office, 1947, pp. 139–148.

"Declaration of Constitutional Principles," *Congressional Record,* 84th Congress, 2d Session, March 12, 1956, pp. 4460–61, 4515–16.

Eisenhower speech: *Public Papers of the President, Dwight David Eisenhower, 1957.* Washington, D.C.: U.S. Government Printing Office, 1958, pp. 689–94.

Hearings before the United States Commission on Civil Rights, Voting, Montgomery, Alabama, December 8, 9, 1958, January 9, 1959. Washington, D.C.: U.S. Government Printing Office, 1959, pp. 75–79, 106–8.

"The FBI and Martin Luther King, Jr.": *Martin Luther King, Jr., FBI File* (microfilm), ed. David Garrow. Frederick, Md.: University Publications of America, 1984. Reprinted by permission.

Kennedy speech: *Public Papers of the President, John F. Kennedy, 1963.* Washington, D.C.: U.S. Government Printing Office, 1964, pp. 468–71.

Wiley Branton letter: courtesy of the Voter Education Project and Southern Regional Council.

Johnson speech: *Public Papers of the President, Lyndon B. Johnson, 1965.* Washington, D.C.: U.S. Government Printing Office, 1966, pp. 281–87.

Report of the National Advisory Commission on Civil Disorders. Washington, D.C.: U.S. Government Printing Office, 1968.

216   *Acknowledgments*

King speech: *A Testament of Hope: The Essential Writings and Speeches of Martin Luther King, Jr.*, ed. James Melvin Washington. San Francisco: HarperSanFrancisco, 1991, pp. 245–52. Reprinted by permission. License granted by Intellectual Properties Management, Atlanta, Georgia, as exclusive Licensor of the King Estate.

"Bigger Than a Hamburger," *The Southern Patriot*, June 1960.

Handbill: *Nonviolence in America,* ed. Staughton Lynd. Indianapolis, Ind.: Bobbs-Merrill, 1965.

Chronology of violence: Papers of the Highlander Education and Research Center, State Historical Society of Wisconsin.

Editorial, cartoon, and poster: *Student Voice.*

Eldridge W. Steptoe, Jr. interview: Center for Oral History and Cultural Heritage at the University of Southern Mississippi, interview by Jimmy Dykes, November 1995. Reprinted by permission.

Fannie Lou Hamer interview: Center for Oral History and Cultural Heritage at the University of Southern Mississippi, interview by Neil McMillen, 1972. Reprinted by permission.

INDEX

Acheson, Dean, 55
ACMHR. *See* Alabama Christian
Movement for Human Rights
activism, 18–19, 118, 129–35, 136.
See also activists; organizing
activists: aggressive, 117; Black soldiers
as, 7; evolution of, 135; grassroots,
2; methods of, 122–23; organizers
of, 127, 141–42; reprisals against,
136–37; students as, 18–19,
129–35; as subversives, 9; women
as, 128. *See also* activism; organizing
actors, 2, 127–28
Adams, Eugene W., 75–78
affirmative action, 39–40, 42
aggression, 54, 117
Alabama Christian Movement for
Human Rights (ACMHR), 123
Albany (Ga.), 22–24, 45, 79–81,
130–31
Albany Movement, 23
Algebra Project, 170, 173–74
Allen, Louis, 142
Anderson, William, 23
assembly, freedom of, 97

Baker, Ella J.: democracy and, 146;
history, absence from, 124; on

King, Martin Luther, Jr., 151; lead-
ership and, 119–22, 171; in Missis-
sippi, 137; organizing and, 182,
186–87; SNCC and, 130, 141,
159; on social struggle, 152; student
activism and, 18–19
Barnett, Ross, 26
Bates, Daisy, 16
Belmont, Alan H., 79
Bernhard, Berl I., 79
Birmingham (Ala.), 26–27, 123, 154
Black Panthers, 38, 39, 43, 44, 122
Black Power, 33–35, 38, 44–45, 147.
See also power
bombings, 26, 27, 123–24, 136
Bond, Julian, 124
boycotts, 13–14, 45, 123, 127–29,
133. *See also* demonstrations
Branton, Wiley A., 88
breach of the peace, 163–65
Britt, Travis, 138, 164
Brotherhood of Sleeping Car Porters,
5, 122, 127
Brown v. Board of Education, 11, 41, 60,
116
Brown, H. Rap, 43
Brownell, Herbert, 14
Bryant, Curtis C., 164, 183
Bryant, William Cullen, 113
Bunche, Ralph J., 116

and, 130; legal status of, 117, 122;
Little Rock school desegregation
and, 16; March on Washington
and, 28, 134; problems in, 120–21;
Steptoe, E. W., and, 189, 190,
196–97; survival of, 39; tactics and,
3–4, 34, 120, 123; Voter Education
Project and, 24
nationalism, 34
National Urban League (NUL), 34, 39
Newton, Huey, 43
Nietzsche, Friedrich, 106
Nixon, E. D., 14, 127
Nixon, Richard M., 19, 39
nonviolence: abandonment of, 34;
commitment to, 18, 121, 143, 160,
161–62; effectiveness of, 132–33;
King, Martin Luther, Jr., and,
43–44, 108–9; organizing and,
177, 180–81; self-defense and, 44,
139; Student Non-Violent Coordinating Committee and, 177; undermining, 166. *See also* violence
NUL. *See* National Urban League

oratory, 175–76
organizing, 10, 141–42, 170–87,
189–98. *See also* activism; grassroots efforts
Owens, Webb, 175, 183

Palmer, Hazel, 170–73
parental rights, 60
Parks, Rosa, 13–14, 127–28
passive resistance, 43–44. *See also* nonviolence
Patterson, John, 21, 22
Peacock, Willie, 175
pickets, 123
Plessy v. Ferguson, 11, 60
poll tax, 33, 204

poverty, 35, 36, 107–8, 110–11, 147
Poweledge, Fred, 129
power, 105–8. *See also* Black Power
prejudice, 54–55, 98. *See also* discrimination
presidency, 5–6, 12–13, 41, 66, 67, 68
President's Committee on Civil
Rights, 7–8, 9, 15, 41, 49–57
press. *See* media
principles, 9, 49–57, 82–83, 91. *See
also* morality
Pritchett, Laurie, 23, 45
privilege, 145–46
property, 192
public services, 13–14, 20–22, 28, 29,
54, 127

racism: changing, 8, 131, 152; democracy, conflict with, 8; institutions,
American, and, 115, 125, 133; international, 131; methods for over-
coming, 4, 131–33; as national
problem, 3–4, 94–95, 148; riots, as
cause of, 37
radicalism, 43–44, 45, 125, 126,
147–48. *See also* militancy
Randolph, A. Philip, 5, 8, 28, 122,
124, 127
Reagan, Cordelle, 164
Reeb, James, 32
relief, 54
religion, 126, 141. *See also* churches;
ministers
repression, 117, 136–37
Reuther, Walter, 106
riots, 36–37, 54. *See also* demonstrations
Roberts v. City of Boston, 60
Robinson, Jo Ann Gibson, 14, 128
Robnett, Belinda, 46
Roosevelt, Franklin D., 4, 5, 122

ABOUT THE AUTHORS

STEVEN F. LAWSON is author of *Civil Rights Crossroads: Nation, Community, and the Black Freedom Struggle* (2003); *Running for Freedom: Civil Rights and Black Politics in America Since 1941,* 2nd edition (1997); *In Pursuit of Power: Southern Blacks and Electoral Politics, 1965–1982* (1985); and *Black Ballots: Voting Rights in the South, 1944–1969* (1976). He participated as an adviser to the documentary film series *Eyes on the Prize* and has served as an expert witness on voting rights cases. He has taught at the University of South Florida, the University of North Carolina–Greensboro, and is currently professor of history and faculty director of the Aresty Research Center for Undergraduates at Rutgers, The State University of New Jersey.

CHARLES PAYNE is professor of African American studies and history at Duke University. He is coeditor of *Time Longer Than Rope: A Century of African American Activism, 1850–1950* (2003) and *Teach Freedom: The African American Tradition of Education for Liberation* (forthcoming). He is author of *Getting What We Ask For: The Ambiguity of Success and Failure in Urban Education* (1984) and *I've Got the Light of Freedom: The Organizing Tradition in the Mississippi Civil Rights Movement* (1995). The latter has won awards from the Southern Regional Council, *Choice* Magazine, the Simon Wiesenthal Center and the Gustavus Myers Center for the Study of Human Rights in North America. Currently, Payne is studying the processes by which failing urban schools get better and he is working on an anthology on grassroots African American activism between the mid-nineteenth and mid-twentieth century. Before joining Duke's faculty, Payne taught at Northwestern University, Williams College, and Southern University.